# Land of the Long White Cloud

## A journey around New Zealand

## – LESLEY GOULD –

An environmentally friendly book printed and bound in England by
www.printondemand-worldwide.com

**Mixed Sources**
Product group from well-managed
forests, and other controlled sources
www.fsc.org  Cert no. TT-COC-002641
© 1996 Forest Stewardship Council
FSC

PEFC Certified
This product is
from sustainably
managed forests
and controlled
sources
www.pefc.org
PEFC
PEFC/16-33-416

This book is made entirely of chain-of-custody materials

*Lesley Gould*

*Many thanks to Peter and Trish for their hospitality and suggestions of places to visit.*

www.fast-print.net/store.php

Land of the Long White Cloud – A journey around
New Zealand
Copyright © Lesley Gould 2012

ISBN 978-178035-410-1

First published 2012 by
FASTPRINT PUBLISHING
Peterborough, England.
Printed by Printondemand-Worldwide

*Lesley Gould*

# *Contents*

*Lesley Gould*

# *Introduction*

This book came about quite by accident. I like to write about my holidays and by doing so get to live them over again. After a great holiday I am inspired to create a scrapbook and account of places we have been with information, photographs, ticket stubs etc. It is a way of remembering all the little things and places that can easily be forgotten over time and is great to look at several years later. This time however there was so much we had seen and done that was stunning and inspiring that I found myself wanting to find out lots more about the places we had seen and how they came about. There were artists we had come across that we wanted to know more about, places that we had seen and places we hadn't had time to get to. The different vegetation, the customs, the past and the present all fascinated me. New Zealand was a land full of stories, myths and legends, matched with a vast variety of landscapes. It was a land of contrasts with each scene having a beauty and character of its own. I imagine it is totally different depending on the season. It was finding out more about these things that led to the creation of this book.

So why did we go to New Zealand in the first place?

I'm not really sure how that came about either! I was about to retire and that would leave Jeff (my husband) and I with no ties in terms of work commitments. We had always said that when we had both retired we would go to Australia as that is where Jeff had emigrated when he was 21, and the idea was that we would revisit some of the places he remembered and see how they had changed. We had done this when we returned to Singapore a few years ago, spending time looking up Jeff's old haunts. We briefly thought about visiting both Australia and New Zealand but were swayed by our daughter and son in law who had loved New Zealand when they went there as part of their honeymoon. So we finally decided on five weeks touring the two islands.

We wanted to be able to go when it was summer in the southern hemisphere and for a reasonable length of time. Anyway we somehow started talking about New Zealand and perhaps visiting my brother (Peter), who now lived over there. Dozens of brochures later and after many hours on the Internet comparing prices and reviews we had booked flights and were now down to the nitty-gritty of thinking about an itinerary.

Our daughter and son in law were full of all the adrenaline fuelled activities they had taken part in. While not all of these appealed some of the places they had visited sounded idyllic in terms of walking trails, scenery, countryside etc. Considering ourselves fairly outdoorsy sort of people there seemed a lot on offer. We wanted to keep costs down but also wanted to feel that we had made the most of our time over there. Originally we planned to just tour North Island and get a real feel about it but I also kept thinking I couldn't go all that way and not see Milford Sound and Fiordland. So the plan changed to incorporate this after visiting North Island, by flying down to Queenstown and driving our way back up the west coast. This would mean we would get to see both Fiordland and the spectacular West and Abel Tasman coastlines.

Like most people we had looked at and compared many flight companies and prices, we had read reviews until we were blue in the face, but found that one company appeared to be best value and with very good reviews, that was Korean Air. We were open minded about where we might stop en route as we had no plans to extend the holiday with a several night stopover. The flights we finally booked meant that we got a night in Seoul included in the flight prices to fit in with the

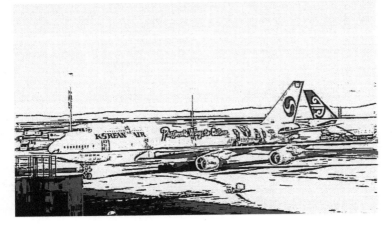

connecting flights. This gave us chance to break the journey home and to get a snapshot of South Korea.

So the flight was booked and now we had to think about our route and itinerary. As we had family in North Island we thought a good way to split the holiday was to stay with them on the way south and then again on our way back to Auckland at the end of our holiday. We thought two shorter stays with family and travelling in between would enable us to catch breath, get some insight on visits etc. However the resting bit never came to pass as they had planned so many brilliant things for us to do during our stay.

As most international flights go into Auckland airport we decided to start there, work our way south through north Island, then fly down from Wellington to Queenstown. We could then work our way back up the west coast, cross back to North Island on the ferry, visit family and end up back in Auckland. This was the plan but we had about 6 variations for "The Plan" depending on which places we decided to visit. This got changed regularly as we talked to people who had already been there, read books and consulted with my brother. The other difficulty we had, in fact the other difficulties we had were;

- How long to stay in each place – depending on what we wanted to do there

- How to travel – own or public transport, car or campervan

- What type of accommodation to use and

- How much to book in advance and how much to leave flexible.

So the blank page was actually a book full of notes and scribbles and mileages. Working out how far was reasonable to travel in a day was also quite difficult. The easy part was that we have similar interests, we both enjoy walking and we are both interested in the history of New Zealand so information and places connected with early settlers, gold mining, Maori culture, fabulous scenery and Lord of the Rings associations were always good bets. Zorbing, looping the loop and white water rafting were not really what we were about. You will by now have recognised that we are not young backpackers but visitors of a more mature age.

We wanted a base in the areas we were planning to visit from where we could walk or drive to the major sights, not too large and at a reasonable price. We chose a real variety of accommodation types with apartments, lodges, hotels, motels and bed and breakfast homes. Not one of the places we booked did we find disappointing, and most were better than expected. We knew it was going to be a fairly expensive break but the weak pound and the longer break meant it was more expensive than we had originally envisioned, however many of the high points of the trip didn't cost money but just needed time.

So we were off to Aotearoa. This is the most widely known and accepted Maori name for New Zealand. It is used by both Maori and non-Maori, and is becoming increasingly widespread. Its original derivation of Aotearoa is not known for certain but it can be broken up into: ao = cloud, tea = white and roa = long, which is where "the land of the long white cloud" comes from.

# *Arrival in Auckland*

So we were going to arrive in Auckland. What was the recommended sightseeing there? We had copies of about 10 different travel books on New Zealand borrowed, bought or given. I must say at this point that one of our best pre holiday planning buys was a lot off eBay that Jeff secured. For less than £5 we had a road atlas with mileage, estimated times for travelling and town plans, several national park large scale maps, a book on tramping in NZ and other smaller leaflets. The atlas has been in constant use for six months and was really useful while over there.

Auckland is New Zealand's largest city and approximately 401,500 people live within the city boundary and 1.25 million in the greater Auckland area. This is about one third of the whole population of New Zealand. The Auckland area was home to Maori people for a thousand years before Europeans settled here. Over 181 different ethnic groups from all over the world call

Auckland home, making it an exciting place to live. Although English is the main language Maori, Polynesian and Asian languages are also spoken by ethnic communities.

Three quarters of all New Zealanders are of European descent, called Pakeha in Maori. The Maori themselves account for approximately 15% of the population.

Auckland City lies on a narrow strip of land between the interesting Manukau and Waitemata harbours and is surrounded by extinct volcanoes and picturesque islands. The Hauraki Gulf and its islands (65 of them), are recognised as a regional and national treasure with their diverse landscapes. Auckland is known as the City of Sails and ownership of recreational boats is the world's highest per capita.

Our arrival in Auckland was at 8.30am. On arrival you have to have filled in an immigration form part of which is declaring any walking and camping gear. A word of

information here, if you are planning on going walking in NZ and taking walking boots they are very strict about making sure these items are clean and that you are not bringing any germs and diseases into the country. My brother had warned us about this prior to coming. New Zealand relies heavily on its agricultural industries and every effort is made to keep the country free of introduced pests and diseases that could jeopardise the productivity of its farms and orchards. Failure also to declare quarantine items such as fruit and plant material can lead to a fine of 100,000 NZ dollars or five years in jail. So when we got to immigration we had to open the cases so the walking boots and poles could be inspected. A very pleasant official was impressed with how clean they were, but then he didn't have to repack the cases.

So having arrived on an early flight we set off in a taxi and arrived at the Rendezvous Hotel at nine forty five in the morning and were amazed that the room was ready and available. Although we had hoped for this, we had expected only to drop off the luggage and return later. Having been travelling for 36 hours this was the best news we could have had. The room was great, spacious, airy and a lovely view over the city.

However this was soon to become eclipsed by a couple of dramatic events;

1. Jeff had lost his waterproof jacket

2. Credit card crisis!

Having unpacked I innocently asked where the said jacket was? Certainly not in the hotel room . We decided it could have been put down when we had to open the cases, or following this when everything had to be scanned again on entry to Auckland, or in the taxi we took to the hotel!

The staff at the hotel were very helpful in phoning the taxi company and we phoned airport lost property but to no avail. So we now needed to buy a new jacket as five weeks without rain seemed too much to ask for.

Travel Tip: make sure all walking/camping gear is spotless because they will check it at the airport, and have it near the top of your case ready for inspection.

We decided what we need next was a cup of tea and to check the emails and let family know that we and arrived safely. I opened our mailbox on our new iPad, (a Christmas present from our children so we could keep in touch while away). I was just starting to relax when I spotted it - the dreaded email!!!

I was looking at an email from America thanking me for purchasing an air ticket to Buffalo at a cost of several hundred American dollars. This had been sent while we were actually in the air. It's bad enough getting such shocks at home but worse when miles away. So what should we do? We didn't know if one of our credit cards had been used or not. We didn't want to respond to the email and find ourselves with further problems. Due to the time difference we could not phone our bank back home as it was the middle of the night. After several calls to England, various helplines and a call to the airline concerned it appeared it was a scam email that several people had received causing the airline a lot of hassle. We hoped this was true and didn't cancel any cards- only just having arrived this could have been a problem for us. We did feel a bit vulnerable for a few days but all was well and fortunately we came home to no unexpected expenditure.

Travel Tip: make sure you have all the numbers you may need regarding banking details etc just in case. We had lots of cards abroad numbers etc but these tend to deal mainly with lost or stolen cards, what we really wanted in addition was simply our local bank number or email.

So after the long flights, the coat debacle and the e-mail crisis, we were feeling rather tired and frazzled but here we were, in Auckland for the long awaited extended holiday. We decided to go for a walk and found Auckland a lovely city. We enjoyed walking round the harbour and the shopping areas.

British settlement in Auckland began in 1820 when Reverend Samuel Marsden named the capital after the Earl of Auckland, George Eden, The Viceroy of India. Marsden arrived on the sailing ship "Coromandel", and this led to a series of land purchases which still cause problems today. It seems likely that the Maori had no concept of land ownership but lived off the land. They probably thought they were accepting gifts to allow people to live on the land. Certainly they didn't make much profit as today one acre of land in the city is worth around twelve million dollars!

It had been recommended that we visit the Victoria Park Market but unfortunately when we went it was closed and in the middle of being refurbished so nowhere

was open. The site was originally a refuse station, and the chimney was used for burning the city's rubbish. In its time ninety-four workhorses were housed in the 'Stables' there. Across the road which is now Victoria Park, was once the beach front. The Historic Places Trust and the Auckland City Heritage Department have restored the buildings to their former glory with a twenty million dollar renovation. Many new shops and restaurants were due to open along with cafes and restaurants in early 2012.

We did enjoy the walk around though and were rewarded with some great views of Auckland Harbour Bridge. By chance we went to the City Art Gallery as we passed it on our way back to our hotel. It is in a lovely airy building with outside exhibits as well as inside. There were lots of paintings and photographs that reflected New Zealand's cultural and creative history over the years. Upstairs there were fabulous portraits of Maori and Pakeha including "A View in Dusky Bay" which is thought to be the earliest oil painting of Maori. The New

Zealand collection contains work from many of the nation's most prominent artists. I particularly liked the modern Maori work by artists such as Para Matchitt who were making modern designs from the traditional styles. There was free entry into the gallery and it is well worth having a couple of hours there.

The following day we took the ferry from the harbour over to Devonport. The ferry is easy and runs every half hour from Auckland's Ferry Building. In ten minutes you find yourself transported to Victoria Wharf, an historic seaside village. There are good views of Auckland Harbour and particularly the Ferry Building as you cross over to Devonport. This was our first experience of how different the houses  are over there in New Zealand, the single storey, wood built Victorian style. These buildings we were to see in all their variations over the next few weeks. The shops are in old heritage buildings and are mainly independent so the range of products is both different and unique. It is a good place if you are looking to find something special to take home.

Devonport was originally an island joined to the mainland by a narrow causeway. Maori settlement here goes back to around the 14th century. It has three small mountains; Takapuna, Takarunga and Takaroa. These were all originally Maori sites. Fishing and shipbuilding were both important here in the past. It was named after the Devonport naval base in England and has a long military history. If you go onto the i-Site on Victoria Road you can get a copy of "The Old Devonport Walk". This takes about an hour to do but introduces you to lots of

interesting old buildings and information about their history.

We only had this one night left in Auckland and really wanted to go up the Sky Tower later in the day so we could get some good views of the sun setting, however there was a lot of cloud about so not quite as planned. It is well worth going up though for the 360 degree views. The tower is 328 metres high, over 1076 feet. It is the tallest structure in the southern hemisphere and is visited by almost one million people a year. It has the Orbit revolving restaurant, the Observatory buffet restaurant and the Sky lounge cafe and bar. While we were there, on the ground floor was the Weta Cave with lots of Lord of the Rings collectables and life size models. It was interesting coming face to face with Gollum and an Orc!   I believe this is only there for a limited time though. For thrill seekers it also has a Vertigo Climb and Sky Jump!

Travel Tip: you get a good reduction here for seniors.

In the evening we went out to eat in the town. Away from the harbour a good spot was  Aotea Square off Queen Street. We spent a pleasant evening sitting outside the Aotea Centre enjoying a light meal and people watching.

We enjoyed Auckland and although there is a lot more to see we were pleased with our choices.

So we had left England on Tuesday and because of the time difference it was now already Saturday and we were setting off for Paihia.  We had arranged for the car to be delivered to the hotel so we didn't need to get downtown to pick up the car that morning but could set off when ready.

We stocked up on one of the Rendezvous' great breakfasts while chatting to the waitress about our visit to Devonport as that was where she lived. We also had an interesting chat with a family who were moving to

Auckland and were staying a couple of nights at the hotel while they got their home ready. Unfortunately he was on crutches as he had snapped his Achilles tendon – that was also a good talking point as I had snapped mine nine years ago. We were to meet over the course of the holiday many interesting people from all over the world and all walks of life.

We had one last thing to do before leaving and that was to Skype our granddaughter back in England. As 8 am in the morning in New Zealand was like 7 pm at home we had arranged to speak to her before her bedtime. There is a thirteen hour time difference during their summer. We were worried she might forget us as we were going to be away for a long while in her terms. (We needn't have worried she was really excited to see us again and I think the Skyping helped us more than her).

# *Northland*

Today we had 150 miles or 241 kilometres to travel up to Paihia in the Bay of Islands. The good thing about driving over there is that everything is just like in England, gears in the right place, passengers in the right place etc etc which makes it much easier. The only thing to remember is that funny rule about yielding to all traffic crossing or approaching from the right - but I am told that is being phased out anyway.

One of the items we found most expensive when booking was the cost of car hire. We needed to have three separate cars and tried various ways of getting better deals. One of the problems was that for each hire most of the companies wanted to block the excess off our credit card which was 3,000 NZ dollars. We were worried that if they did this three times without refunding immediately we could be short of funds. It was not a continuous hire as we did not need a car when we were in the cities. Of course one way to avoid these charges is to take out additional cover and the excess is then drastically reduced.

We did read that if you were staying longer than two months it was probably cheaper to buy a second hand car and then sell it again at the end of the holiday. We didn't check out car prices so can't verify this. All I can say is that it seemed a lot of money at the time.

Having said this, all our cars were through Avis New Zealand and each car was less than a year old and with very low mileage. The company were efficient and helpful although the database didn't carry details forward and we had to give all our details each time which seemed a bit ludicrous! Overall though we were happy with both the cars and the service.

<u>Travel Tip:</u> There were bargains on the web and it does pay to look at several companies as there are many out there. Also all bookings don't have to be with the same company.

Thoroughly explore all the different rates and companies and look out for special offers.

We had our car and we set off over the Auckland Harbour Bridge which arches across Waitemata Harbour to the North shore suburbs. The bridge is over 1km long. When it opened in 1959 it had four lanes and now has eight. There are great views of the harbours and the Sky Tower from the bridge.

Not long out of Auckland we came across the Northern Gateway Toll Road. This is a 7.5 km motorway extension. Heading north, the toll road begins just before Orewa and ends after the Johnstone Hills near Puhoi. You are warned of the option of taking the scenic coastal route north or the new toll road. We were keen to get up north sooner rather than later so opted for the toll road. You then have options of how to pay (there are no toll booths). You can pay by phone, on the Internet or stop at the next services and pay at the machine. We thought the machine sounded easy so stopped only to find the queue to pay stretched right across the service station. There were two machines though, well there were at first! At some point in the wait men came to empty a machine and couldn't get it to work again. So 40 minutes later we have paid for that journey and the return just in case! It seemed a long wait to pay a toll of only 2.20 NZ dollars. The amount you pay depends on the type of vehicle you are driving and is being increased from March 1st 2012. The daft thing was that when we returned we took the scenic route for the views but also saw the toll machine by the roadside with only one person there. According to the website tolls should be paid before you travel but you can pay up to five days after before receiving a toll payment notice which will contain a $4.90 administration charge in addition to the toll.

Travel tip: pay tolls by phone if possible.

After leaving the motorway you are down to single lane roads for the rest of the journey. In fact it was something we noticed that most of the roads were single lane, we only found dual carriageways near to the big cities. Also there was usually only one road to where you were going so it is actually quite hard to get lost. We were really glad we didn't pay for a Sat Nav system. The roads generally were quiet, though we did get held up at Wellsford which seemed to be a bit of a bottleneck. The speed limit is 100km/h on the open road and 50 km/h in urban areas. Speed cameras are scattered throughout the country and we noticed lots of police cars as we travelled even in very remote areas. We had read that excessive speed is a major hazard in New Zealand but we did not experience this at all and felt that drivers generally were much less aggressive than in England.

Travel Tip: although not a large country, because it is very hilly the roads wind a lot. Roads away from towns are all single lane, therefore it can take much longer than expected to get to your destination.

We stopped off at Ruakaka beach as it wasn't far off the route for a break and view. There are some great views here across Urquarts Bay to the mountains. A little further on we stopped at the i-Site at Whangarei. This was a good spot for lunch and lots of information about the area we were heading to.

We had booked an apartment in Paihia having viewed masses of websites back home. It was an awesome apartment, lots of light and space, a fully equipped kitchen area, large bed, separate bathroom with washing machine too. We had our own decking in the garden looking out over the bay. It had huge windows on two sides to take in the views and was set in the owners garden hence its name "the garden suite". There were lots of birds and it was here that we heard our first Tui, a sound that we came to recognise instantly and often over the holiday. The owner was very friendly and helpful and we had arranged to have continental breakfast which was delivered to the room the night before so we could have it at whatever time we wanted. The place was set back from the main town so it was quiet which suited us and yet only a 10 minute walk down into Paihia when we went out.

To many people Paihia is known for the hole in the rock cruise and we did fancy both this or possibly the cream trip. Our problem is that we love exploring on foot and New Zealand has some of the best tramping trails going. We had two full days and we wanted to go to the Waitangi treaty grounds and have a look round Paihia itself. So next morning when we could tear ourselves away from the view and breakfast on the deck, we set off on a short walk to the Paihia lookout. We had found the details of this on the Internet before going out there. It is described as a pleasant walk through regenerating native forest to a lookout with stunning views over Waitangi, Bay of Islands and Russell. It is 1.5kms each way on an easy track. It starts 700metres from the town at the top of School Road. Having found the start it was well marked as were all the walks we did. We only saw one other couple on the whole of the walk and the views were great. The couple were our age and lived in New Zealand but each year came up to the Bay of Islands for a holiday. This was one of their regular walks.

In the afternoon we took the ferry over to Kororareka, otherwise known as Russell. The town's original Maori name means "sweet penguin". Legend has it that a wounded Maori chief after being given some penguin soup uttered "Ka-reka- te-korora", meaning how sweet is the penguin.

Passenger and car ferries cross to Russell from Paihia regularly throughout the day and evening. It was a quiet seaside village and very popular for people with boats and yachts. Heritage trail leaflets are available from the i-Site. Earlier in its history it was a shore station for whalers, sealers and escaped convicts, becoming a lawless town and earning the title "hell hole of the pacific". It is hard to believe that this was New Zealand's largest town before 1840. It is now a sleepy village very much revolving around tourism and fishing. Away from the waterfront in the heart of Russell is the museum. Although small it is packed with information and I'm glad we didn't miss it out. It has an interesting collection of relics belonging to early settlers and an impressive 1:5 scale replica of Captain Cooks ship "The Endeavour". It's open every day except Christmas day.

Each year the Russell Boat Club hosts the annual Tall Ships and Classics Regatta in January in the Bay of Islands. This was its 37th year and it had taken place just before we were out there. I had read reports about it in the news just before we set off. Apparently the weather had been terrible with heavy winds and driving rain. It certainly separated the masters from the novices being the worst possible conditions for sailing these large ships. Many people had thought it the worst weather the Tall Ships Race had ever seen. The swell and wind from the south-east created conditions too rough for some of the square riggers and they remained moored along with about half of the 60 boats which would have lined up for the races had the weather been better. Ten boats finished the Tall Ships race, with the yacht Black Panther taking first place and fifteen boats finished the Classic Invitation race. The Race Day ends with a huge Hangi meal to celebrate the victors. This is the traditional feast of the Maori people, all cooked in a massive underground pit.

The other visit we wanted to make from here was to the Waitangi Treaty Ground. The Treaty of Waitangi is New Zealand's founding document. It is the agreement between the Maoris and the British Government that is now the centrepiece of the country's race relations. The majority but not all the Maori chiefs signed the document but misunderstandings arose because there were two different versions (Maori and English), which carried different meanings. Dispute over the Treaty continues to this day. Waitangi Day, a bank holiday is celebrated each year on February 6th.

Entry to the Treaty Ground was through the reception centre at the main entrance. Within the grounds is the Treaty House, the Flagstaff where the treaty was first signed, a Maori war canoe and a Maori Meeting House.

The Maori Waka (canoe), is housed in a shelter on Hobsons Beach. The 35 metre long Ngatokimatawhaorua was made from three massive kauri trees from the Puketi forest. A minimum of 76 paddlers are needed to handle it safely on the water. It is very impressive and near it by the beach was a reconstruction of a Maori settlement.

The Te Whare Runanga or meeting house was opened in 1940 during the Centenary Celebrations. It is a typical meeting house but is unique in that it was planned to be shared by all the Maori tribes. There is lots of space to wander around the grounds and beach, also a cafe, theatre and visitor centre where you can book different types of tours or watch cultural performances. Within the grounds there is also a coastal walk that takes you past unusual lava rocks.

From Waitangi we walked along the Mangrove Forest Boardwalk which took us through a Kiwi habitat (but we didn't see any), and mature mangrove forest to Haruro Falls at the end of the tidal Waitangi River. It is a sheltered walk starting from the Treaty Grounds at Waitangi through the bush-clad banks of the river. The walk is 6kms each way. At first it followed the edge of the Waitangi Golf Course, then followed the river for most of its length, passing through some unusual and attractive native trees. A feature of the walk is the boardwalk section which leads through the interior of a mature

mangrove forest, an area which would be inaccessible normally. There are information boards about the Mangrove and its ability to live in salt water.

As you near Haruru Falls, the river widens. There are lots of nests in the pohutukawa trees which overhang the river. The Pohutukawa tree is possibly one of the best known New Zealand native trees. Pohutukawa flowers are bright red, smothering the tree in December, hence its common name: the New Zealand Christmas Tree.

Getting closer to the destination we heard the thundering roar of Haruru Falls. Haruru means "big noise". In the 1800's there were over a hundred Maori villages near here. The wide basin below the falls is interesting as it was New Zealand's first river port and an important transport junction in the early days of European settlement. Today it is a popular holiday spot with resort hotels and holiday parks around its perimeter.

Before going back to our apartment we drove up to Kerikeri but only had time for a brief look round. Kerikeri is home to the Stone Store, New Zealand's oldest surviving stone building and the Kerikeri Mission House the oldest surviving wooden house. Just across the river is Rewa's Village. This is a recreation of a Maori fishing settlement or Kainga with the basic Ponga tree fern huts. Kerikeri  is also famous for its citrus and kiwi fruit orchards.

We had enjoyed Paihia and reflected (over some Picton Bay Sauvignon Blanc and watching the sunset), that we had done quite a lot in the two days we were there even though we hadn't managed to fit in a boat trip other than the ferry.

<u>Travel Tip</u>: Find out about the Ponga

You cannot read any further without knowing something about New Zealand's national symbol, the native tree fern. The Maori word for silver fern is 'ponga'.

The leaves are dark green at the top and silvery at the bottom, hence the name silver fern. Many sports teams use the silver fern symbol, the All Blacks, the Tall Blacks, the Silver Ferns, the Black Caps, the Black Sticks, Team New Zealand and many other teams. The koru is a favourite shape, the koru is the Maori name for the fern frond which unfurls into the leaf. The koru symbolises new life, new beginnings, growth and movement. There are ten species of tree fern in New Zealand and eight of them are specific to the country. Ponga are a special feature of the New Zealand bush. The largest is the Black Ponga or Mamaku Ponga which grows to about twenty metres.

There is no way you can miss the pongas because they are everywhere.

# *Central North Island*

The next part of our route was to head south and get past Auckland so that we only had a short drive to Rotarua the following day. Doing it this way we had time to stop off at any interesting places and sites as we drove

back south. Our first stop off was only a short distance away but is mentioned in many of the tourist guides, the famous public toilets in Kawakawa, otherwise known as Hundertwasser's Loo. They were well signed from the highway but we missed them somehow as we drove through the town and had to ask. Frederick Hundertwasser was an artist born in Austria and he designed these toilets in Kawakawa. They are said to be the most original in New Zealand. Certainly they were original. It is a work of art made from coloured tiles, windows made from wine bottles and not a straight line anywhere. It has bulbous pillars at the front which is probably why we didn't recognise it, and it has a grass roof. The artist died in 2000.

When we got to the toll road again we decided not to go on it this time but to take the scenic coastal route which took us through Waiwera, Hatfields Beach and Orewa. There are some lovely views along this road, especially as you drop down towards the beach.

Getting through Auckland was easy, Highway 1 takes you straight through without any turn offs so little chance of getting lost. There are some great views of Auckland Harbour and the Sky Tower as you approach the city.

We had planned to stop at a small place called Te Kauwhata where we had found an interesting bed and breakfast. It was 200 miles from Paihia which taking the roads and a leisurely pace into account seemed a good distance. It looked a good place to relax with the added promise of tea and scones on arrival which appealed. It was a real find. What we hadn't realised was that it was a very fashionable boutique bed and breakfast with a reputation for a quiet getaway and was often very busy. It was only 1 kilometre off Highway 1 in a rural setting offering total tranquility. We had tea with both lavender and dates with rosemary scones. They were delicious; all served in a Devonshire High Tea fashion, the cake stand also being adorned with fresh flowers.

Trish the owner explained how she came to be running a guest house, herb garden, bread making classes etc. Several of her family were now also engaged in the venture which had started when she wanted to make sure her young family ate well, thus getting into bread making and baking. Hers was quite a story. Twenty years ago the Budd Family moved to the dairy farm in Te Kauwhata, a small country village within the heart of the Waikato. Trish had always had a romantic vision of a small cottage surrounded by a herb garden. Using a derelict cottage on the property she was able to fulfil this dream, with the help of husband Ian and family of five . This became the business known as Herb Haven, these products eventually led on to the exclusive gift line Baytree & Budd.

Baytree & Budd's commitment is to have an exquisitely packaged gift line which not only looks fantastic, but brings flavours reminiscent of decades ago in Grandma's kitchen. The foods here are made without preservatives, additives or colouring, and made in small batch quantities. Herb Haven products are sold to stores throughout New Zealand and also to Australia and New York.

The business quickly became too large for the small cottage as they were becoming one of the largest Herb Gardens in New Zealand. An old villa was then relocated to reside adjacent to the garden. This was refurbished and became the new home of "Herb Haven".

The business became renowned for the unique experience of guided garden tours accompanied by Victorian teas. Herb teas and lavender scones are still served with specialty jams and cream with edible flowers and presented on antique cake stands and we can vouch for how delicious they are!

A high point in this success was when Trish was awarded the ultimate professional women's business accolade in 1995—the "New Zealand Woman in Business" award. Trish's son Sean now markets the products from the Baytree and Budd range. Trish continues to run the B and B among other ventures, and daughter Rowena, one of five siblings, assists with the business.

The villa is now operating as the boutique Herb Garden Bed & Breakfast, from which the products can still be purchased, and what a lovely place it was. You can choose from the Rose, Lily or Lavender rooms. They are all different with pure cotton sheets, a spacious lounge and dining area with large verandas overlooking the garden and rural views. There are complimentary port and chocolates in the rooms and the toiletries of course are herb based. It was a brilliant place to relax.

So you see it was rather a good find. After the excellent breakfast complete with flowers we only had about 100 miles to do the following morning.

We set off down Highway 1 past Huntly, then turning off onto Highway 1B through to Cambridge where we found a lovely coffee stop with free fill ups. Cambridge sits on the Waikato River and is so called because its tree lined streets and village green give it a very English atmosphere. It is a major centre for the horse breeding industry. It is here that you find " New Zealand Horse Magic". They have a variety of horse breeds including a Lippizaner stallion, Arabian, Clydesdale and the New Zealand wild horse the Kaimaniwa.

We also passed near to Matamata where you can still visit the set of Hobbiton from Lord of the Rings fame. The home of Bag End is set on private land and can only be visited for a fee. There are lots of interesting facts to be gleaned though such as the one about the large oak tree that overlooked Bag End. This  was actually brought in from nearby.  It was cut up, each branch numbered and was then reconstructed and bolted back together for when it was required. We left Matamata for now though as we did not know what other sites we may visit from the films.

Arriving  in Rotarua in the early afternoon we found our room was waiting for us. We had chosen the Victoria Lodge Motel. It was set back away from the lake and the rooms were compact but we knew this when we booked. We had chosen it for three reasons:

- they served breakfast in your room

- it was reasonably priced

- each room had its own thermal pool.

In fact although compact it was exceptionally clean, had plenty of hanging space, fridge, microwave, table to eat at etc. so perfectly adequate. The owners as we had come to expect now were extremely helpful, cheerful and chatty.

We spent the afternoon that day walking around Rotorua, by the lake, looking at the buildings and getting a feel for the town while contemplating what we wanted to do on our full day there and where to eat that night. It was a very hot day and we decided to treat ourselves to a private pool at the Polynesian Spa. Overlooking Lake Rotorua, the Spa is a place where you can relax in one of many hot mineral spring pools or indulge in some of the spa therapies.

It all started when in 1878 a catholic priest found that his arthritis was much better after bathing in the thermal waters of hand-dug pools where the Polynesian Spa is now located. So began an international reputation for the therapeutic properties of the spring water. Shallow-spring hot acidic water supplies the therapeutically renowned Priest Spa and soothing, deep-spring hot alkaline water supplies all the other pools.

We opted for the privacy of our own hot mineral rock pool. The pools temperature was 39 degrees centigrade and we had panoramic views over Sulphur Bay on Lake Rotorua - what a treat!

On returning to the motel and a chat with our hosts, they booked for us a visit to Hells gate the following day and a Maori feast and Matariki Show for the evening.

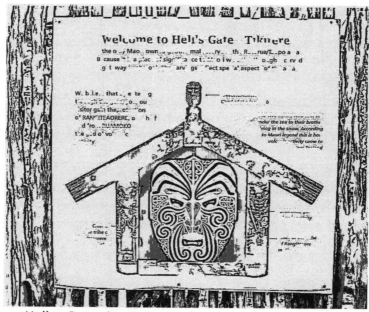

Hells Gate is New Zealand's only Maori owned thermal park and is therefore very important to the Ngati Rangiteaorere tribe who have been at this unique site for more than 700 years. New Zealand as a country is located on the "ring of fire", the earth constantly moving. This is very evident on Rotorua's volcanic plateau with its geysers, fumeroles, mud pools and hot thermal waters. The Maori name for this particular thermal park is Tikitere. The reason it is known widely as Hells Gate is because George Bernard Shaw on visiting the area, when he saw the thermal activity decided this must be the gateway to hell.

The experience includes a guided or self guided walk, 2.5 kilometres of natural geothermal park, native bush, mud foot pool, Maori carving experience, on site cafe and souvenir shop. We decided to guide ourselves as there was a really comprehensive leaflet of information to explain the sights along the way. We enjoyed the mud foot pool and both made a wood carving which we have brought back home to treasure (or use as a drinks mat).

You start the walk at the Gateway or "Waharoa", that represents their ancestral chief – Rangiteaorere, and the Maori God of volcanic activity, "Ruamoko". It is a wonderful walk by boiling mud pools and cliffs. There is also a bush walk which gives a great contrast to the barren thermal landscape. The foot pool was part of the walk but there are also mud baths and a Spa.

As we had driven out to Hells Gate that morning we noticed on the outskirts of Rotorua a large forest area signed as Redwoods and Whakarewarewa Forest which looked as though it had lots of walking tracks so decided to go and explore that for the afternoon. There was a visitor centre with lots of information about both walking and bike trails. We set off on the Pohaturoa track, a circular walk of 7.5kilometres through the forest and to a great lookout over both Rotorua town and the Whakarewarewa Thermal Village and also to Lake Rotarua in the distance. It was quite a busy area looking at the car park, though we didn't see many people on our trail.

The Whakarewarewa Forest has one of the oldest mountain bike networks in the country. With around 90km of trails, there is something to cater for all levels of rider, from beginners and family groups through to experts looking for extreme action.

The trails all weave their way through lush native ferns beneath the huge forest canopies of Redwood, Radiata, Douglas Fir, Eucalyptus and Larch. Rotorua is renowned among mountain bikers as the location for a huge range of premier mountain biking events such as the 2006 World Mountain Bike & Trails Champs, the Single Speed Nationals in 2008 and the annual 12 and 24 hours Cateye Moonride, Xterra and N-Duro Winter MTB Series to name but a few. All this is just a five minute drive from the city centre. Again this reminded me of Whistler, Canada which is popular with mountain bikers out of the ski season.

Having had a good walk I decided it was good time to try out the in room spa bath. It was great though the water was so hot I had to wait half an hour for it to cool down. That evening we had booked to go to a Hangi feast and Maori show in Rotorua and were being picked up for it from our motel. It was known as "Matariki", a cultural experience in the town, though there are several others around the area.

The evening started with drinks at 6.30pm and we learnt some of Rotorua's history spanning over 150 years. We found ourselves on a table with people  from Italy, Denmark and Switzerland. Other tables were taken up mainly by German and Korean visitors. We had an interesting conversation with our Italian guests who were not sure about David Cameron and where we stood with regards to Europe. We thought it best not to mention Mr Berlosconi and maintain diplomatic relations with the table. It was a very sociable evening though.

As part of the introduction a representative had to accept the fern laid down by the Maori chief to show that the audience come in peace. For some reason Jeff had been asked to perform this task and be the representative of the people present, taking the leaf and showing that we came in peace and rubbing noses with the very animated Maori Chief. I am still not sure if he was asked because he spoke English (not that it was a speaking part) or because of his acting skills. His friends will know the answer to this one!

This acting debut was followed by the lifting of the hangi (Maori food) and the chance to sample the traditionally steamed cooked food prepared in the hangi pit. We were given explanations about how the hangi worked and watched the food being taken out. The food included fish, meat and vegetable dishes, salads, desserts and coffee. The choice was excellent  and there were plenty of seconds! The actual pit used was electric as they are not allowed to use fire within the town boundary.

This was followed by the legends of the local Maori people, and we were then entertained by  traditional songs, the haka, poi dance, stick games and the famous story of Hinemoa and Tutanekai. The legend starts one evening  when Tutanekai and his friend were playing music together on Mokoia Island in the centre of Lake Rororua. The sound of the music drifted across the lake to the beautiful and noble born Hinemoa.  When Tutanekai visited the mainland he met Hinemoa and they fell in love. When it was time for Tutanekai to return to his village he agreed to play his flute and Hinemoa would follow the sound and find him. He started playing that night but Hinemoa's people thought something was wrong and had hidden all the canoes. However undeterred, Hinemoa swam to the island. At that moment Tutanekai sent his servant for some water. Hinemoa pretended to be a man and in a gruff voice asked for some water from a calabash which she smashed when she had drunk her fill. The servant reported back to Tutaneki who sent him back several times with the same results. Angry, Tutaneki finally went to the waters edge himself and found Hinemoa.  It was a happy ever after story.

With the absence of written material, dance and song play a central role in Maori culture, often re-enacting particular scenarios.

The evening ended at about 9pm and we were then taken back by car to our motel .We thought it was really good value for money.  It had been a very busy day and a great evening of entertainment, perhaps touristy but that is what we were. We did feel we had received a rounded and varied insight into what Rotorua had to offer.

The next day we awoke to low cloud and not a good forecast. This was a shame because it was today that we were travelling to Lake Taupo and then through the Tongariro National Park and hoping for some great views of Mount Ruapehu on the way to stay with my brother and his wife Trish.

Just before reaching Taupo we stopped at the  Huka Falls. The Huka Falls are the largest falls on the Waikato River and are the most visited natural attraction in New Zealand. The Waikato river is one of New Zealand's longest rivers and it drains from Lake Taupo which itself is the largest freshwater lake in all of Australasia. At the falls the Waikato River which is normally 100metres wide, is squeezed through a 20 metre wide gorge and over a 20metre drop as it crosses a hard volcanic ledge. Every second up to 220,000 litres of water gushes through the gorge and shoots out over 8 metres beyond to create a beautiful blue/green pool. The name Huka is the Maori word for 'foam'. Huka Falls is located in Wairakei Park a 5 minute drive north of Lake Taupo. We did the 30 minute riverside walk as a way to get to the several viewing platforms that are available.

Taupo itself is a bustling town with interesting shops, cosy cafes and restaurants. It's also great for the little ones as there are plenty of family activities to do in the region. It has many attractions and museums that inform you about the area's colourful culture and history. It also has a tranquil side with its thermal hot pools and spas, quiet walking trails, golf courses, lakeside picnics and of course the beautiful scenic attraction of the Great Lake.

For the more adventurous there are activities such as skydiving, mountain biking, bungy jumping and jet boating can be found all around Great Lake Taupo as well as a full range of water activities.

As mentioned the lake itself is the largest freshwater lake in Australasia and undoubtedly a unique and picturesque area. It was one of the film locations for The Lord of The Rings trilogy and the upcoming The Hobbit movie.We had a lovely stop here for coffee and a browse round some of the shops.

From Taupo the road followed the lake for ages and ages giving a real feel for how big this lake is. It is absolutely massive. The water was choppy but this did not deter the many sailors out on the lake.

Then we continued on to Tongariro. The views and the weather were not to be though, the rain started soon after we left Taupo and the low cloud and drizzle stayed with us throughout the National Park. So this particular sight is high on our list for a future visit perhaps doing the day walk known as the Tongariro crossing.

There are many walks, suitable for most park visitors in and around Tongariro National Park. Walks range from fifteen minutes to trips of four to five days. The information centres provide details on all walks and include a range of brochures.

Tongariro was New Zealand's first national park and a world heritage area. The park was created in 1887 when three volcanoes, Rupapehu, Ngauruhoe and Tongariro, were gifted to the people of New Zealand by Ngati Tuwharetoa, the local iwi (people).

The Grand Chateau, one of New Zealand's most iconic hotels is situated in the Tongariro Park and within a fifteen minutes drive from here you are transported into the heart of Mordor for Lord of the Rings fans. Mount Ruapehu is the highest peak in North Island at 2796 metres. Eruptions during the last century spread ash as far as Welington. The crater itself is acidic and occasionally mud and rock are thrown down the mountainside. The volcanoes are unique because of a combination of three factors: the frequency of eruptions, their highly explosive nature and the high density of active vents. Over the last century the average interval between eruption events for Ruapehu has been less than a year.

On 23rd September 1995 following several months of low to moderate tremors an eruption of steam, lake silt, rocks and ash was seen by thousands of skiers on the two commercial ski fields. Mud flowed down the Whangaehu, Mangaturuturu and Whakapapanui valleys. Gas emissions followed and then Ruapehu went quiet until June 1996 when it dramatically erupted ash, fire fountains and sonic booms. The ash cover closed the two ski fields for a period. It was the only disappointment really that we never saw Ruapehu. It was a wild and windy drive through high moorland areas and very steep and windy roads.

# *Family 1*

However, 193 miles later we arrived in Bulls for a family visit, with the cloud clearing finally and the sun coming out. Bulls the unforget-a-bull. Throughout the town the names of the shops and businesses are a play on the word Bull, so the library is called Read-a-bull etc. A bit of fun but people all knew this about the place when we said we were staying in Bulls. The town is

named after James Bull, who founded the town and owned the first general store there. The town itself is unpretentious but has some lovely, interesting old buildings. Just looking at all the different shop facades, including some lovely art deco ones, gives an insight into how it has grown over the years but actually how little has changed..

We found it easily, as I have already said it is actually quite hard to get lost except perhaps in cities. Their house is a large single storey timber building with plenty of land around it like many houses in New Zealand. Even when they look as though they are brick built it is often only cladding on top of wood. They have no central heating which again is not unusual. We found that wherever we stayed though, apartments, hotels B and B's they all had electric blankets, even though it was summer and hot, presumably because of the general lack of central heating

in most houses. Another aspect of housing over there is that they move houses around. You can go house shopping and buy a particular house and then have it transported to where you want to live. This is not unusual and more like our large static caravan idea. These were much bigger though and were often transported in several pieces. Many of them also have corrugated roofs.

Peter and Trish had no radiators in the house but it didn't seem to be a problem, they had a wood burner that warmed the house, wood being a very plentiful fuel over there. We had got used to seeing lots of small and large wooden houses and baches.

So what is a bach? The term bach (pronounced batch, baches or batches in plural) is used in New Zealand to refer to holiday homes or beach houses. These are also called cribs in Southland. The word bach originates from bachelor pad, but in reality is more of a family holiday home. Many of these hadn't changed much in style since the early settlers and all were different. It was really interesting seeing all the variations from the exquisite to the ones that looked as though they might fall down.

We arrived at Peter and Trish's for our long awaited reunion. We hadn't seen Trish for about twenty five years, Peter though had been to England on business. After a cup of tea and non- stop chat we went out for a short drive and walk.

We drove through Scotts Ferry, a Settlement 19 km south-west of Bulls near the mouth of the Rangitīkei River, named after Thomas Scott who started a ferry service in 1849. The actual ferry site is a restored barge by the river and is a reminder of the importance ferries played in New Zealand in the days before bridges were common. Scott also established a trading post and accommodation house at Parewanui. He entered into agreements with local Maori, trading wheat, Indian corn and pigs.

When the Manawatu and Rangitikei county councils were established they took over the ferry service, continuing to employ Scott as the ferryman. Scott died in January 1892 and his widow, Charlotte, and her son took over the service.

In April 1897 a large flood tore the banks of the river, destroying all bridges in its path and changing the course of the Rangitikei. The port was destroyed and the ferry site washed away. The ferry was eventually restored with government assistance. With the development of alternative forms of transport, including the North Island main trunk railway line (finished 1908), the need to maintain the ferry as a major transport link declined and, despite opposition from local settlers, it was closed in 1907. In 1908 the barge was sold to the Featherstone family at Parikino. The new owners used the barge to transfer stock across the Whanganui River. In the 1970s the barge was taken down the Whanganui River for an intended maritime museum. The museum never happened and the barge gradually sank into the mud of the riverbank. In 1989 the barge was raised and sited according to the New Zealand Historic Places Trust, near the original Scott's Ferry site. Members of the local community undertook its restoration as a 1990 sesquicentennial project.

Today, Scott's Ferry Site is a memorial to a form of transport that was common in New Zealand in the nineteenth century. It was these small town stories that we found really interesting regarding the history of New Zealand and that can't be found in the general tourist books.

Just beyond it lies Moanaroa Beach which is where we went walking.

We walked along the sand dunes to the mouth of the river and then back to the car through the pinewoods. We didn't see a soul on the beach. Prior to protection much of this dune area was stabilised for farming and forestry practices. Strong westerly winds still create large scale sand movement which is a feature of these dune systems, sometimes creating problems for coastal settlements and roads.

The sand dunes of the Manawatu Region are the finest remaining examples of the parabolic dune systems that once covered a far wider area than one can see. These are U shaped mounds of sand due to wind and erosion. However they do create a unique habitat for a special collection of New Zealand's native plants and animals. The poisonous katipo spider dwells on this coast line, hiding well away in tunnels on old driftwood or at the base of dune vegetation. Dotterels lay their eggs along the stony flats, with no protection, making them highly vulnerable to being trampled or driven on. The Dotterel is found only in New Zealand. It was once widespread and common but there are only about 1700 of these birds left. This serious decline in numbers is partly due to losing their natural habitat and the effect of introduced mammals becoming their predators. Driving along beaches is also quite common in New Zealand. I have noticed since returning there are lots of videos on the internet of beach driving over there.

We returned to have our first Kiwi barbeque and an evening tasting different New Zealand wines. Another full day and there was more to follow as Peter and Trish outlined what they had in store for us for the next few days. We were certainly not in for a rest.

The following morning we set off first of all, north to Marton, which is where Peter works. Marton has always been a busy town set in the fertile farming region of the Manawatu Plains. The arrival of the railway in 1878 led to its rapid growth in the area, which soon led to further industries such as engineering, sawmilling and textile production in the town. Marton is the largest town in the Rangitikei district, and began life as a private township in 1866. This means that housing sections and shops were sold at auction.

For a while, as a small village it was known as Tutaenui, which is the name of the stream running through its centre. In 1869 it was changed to Marton which is the name of the village where Captain James Cook was born in Yorkshire, marking his landing in New Zealand exactly 100 years earlier.

From the start Marton was an ideal supply centre for district farmers, who first began arriving in the early 1850s. From butter and wool they moved on to growing wheat in 1863, and big crops led to three flourmills being built in the area in 1864.

The opening of the railway line joining Wanganui to Palmerston North in 1878, now part of the North Island Main Trunk Railway (towards Palmerston North and Auckland) and the Marton - New Plymouth Line (towards

Wanganui), helped turn it into a thriving railway junction. Marton has all the shops and services you would expect from a small town, the population is currently about 7,500. It also holds a country music festival each year.

We then moved on to Turakina on the main highway from Bulls to Wanganui. We were off to visit the 148th Turakina Highland Games. There are many Scottish communities in New Zealand but the Turakina Caledonian Society was established in 1864 and is believed to be the oldest. There were lots of stalls, competitions and activities going on. It was well supported with people from all over New Zealand and has a very comprehensive website reporting the event each year.

Turakina is only a small village in the west of the district. The Maori explorer Hau named Turakina, along with the other rivers on this coast. On his journey south searching for his wife, he used a felled log to cross the river [from "Turaki" - to fell).

The first European settlers arrived here from Scotland in ships from 1840's. They walked up the beach from Wellington following the purchase of land from the Ngati Apa people in May 1849, negotiated by Sir Donald McLean. At its peak in the late 1880's Turakina and the surrounding area supported 3 churches. The state primary school was established in 1852, and the Turakina Maori Girls College was here but is now sited in Marton. Early business was brisk with four hotels but the arrival of the railway that enabled Marton to expand led to a slow decline in the fortunes of the Turakina Village.

The 1980's however saw its fortunes change as new people settled in the village building new houses and renovating and restoring old ones. Today it has many heritage buildings dating from the 1850's. There is an adjacent beach settlement Koitiata (meaning "the rising of the morning sun"). Unfortunately in February 2004 the Turakina Valley was severely flooded.

It was an interesting morning. From here we continued to Wanganui and had a walk along the river and through the town, a much bigger town than Marton and Turankina. The main street is full of restored buildings, with Edwardian style gas lamps, seats, and lots of flowers in planters and hanging baskets. There are lots of speciality stores, antique shops, galleries and craft outlets. A really attractive town. Nearby is also the Trafalgar Square shopping mall.

The Whanganui River Road follows the river from just north of Wanganui to Pipiriki. Following the river road is like stepping back in time, with lots of evidence of early European settlement as well as many historic landmarks and features. This is a fascinating drive for those wanting to experience real New Zealand. I imagine it is what New Zealand was like in those early days. The River Road was opened in 1934 having been delayed many times because of floods and slips. Before this almost all access to these remote settlements up the river was from boats. At Hiruharama there is a beautiful village and convent.

Pipiriki is the end of the Whanganui River Road and from here boat trips are available to the famous 'Bridge to Nowhere'. Many canoe tours start and end here too. The journey from Wanganui to Pipiriki takes 2 to 4 hours, depending on the number of stops and due to its winding nature. The route is also part of the New Zealand Cycleway.

Travel Tip: Find out about routes on the New Zealand Cycleway, we only found out about this by chatting to locals on one of our walks.

The government announced in May 2009 the creation of a new national cycleway that will allow visitors to explore New Zealand's unique wilderness areas and spectacular scenery. The Prime Minister John Key announced the Government would spend $50 million over three years to build a national cycleway.

The initiative would create a series of 'Great Rides' of New Zealand that would have the long term aim of creating a network throughout the country. The idea was to link many existing tracks with new pathways and will allow cyclists into some of New Zealand's most scenic and rarely seen countryside. It has become a long distance route to do for many New Zealanders and also appeals to international tourists who may only want to do a short scenic section and enjoy a different experience.

One of the first tracks to be developed was the Mountain to the Sea / Mt Ruapehu to Wanganui. It starts on the slopes of Mt Ruapehu, the route includes the 294-metre Hapuawhenua viaduct, the Whanganui National Park, the historic Mangapurua Valley and the iconic 'Bridge to Nowhere'.

For people wanting to only do part of the track, many tour operators offer a cycle hire service and can drop off and collect riders from any point. The cycleway is seen as a high quality tourism asset and we certainly saw a lot of cyclists as we were travelling, plus minivans transporting bikes and baggage. It seemed a popular tourist activity. We also saw areas where the route was still under construction, particularly on our route out of Rotarua.

Back to Wanganui and our walk along the river by the Wanganui Riverboat Centre. Moored here is the Paddle Steamer Waimarie. The PS Waimarie was built in 1889 by Yarrow & Co Shipbuilders at Poplar, London, and transported in kit set form to Wanganui.

For almost fifty years she carried cargo, mail, locals and tourists up and down the river. When the river road opened river traffic dwindled and she sank at her berth in 1952. She remained buried in the silt and mud of the River until 1993, when she was salvaged and moved into the Whanganui Riverboat Centre for restoration. Waimarie now runs daily two hour cruises up the river for tourists.

The Wanganui District was first settled by Maori, who were attracted by the Whanganui River in its sheltered fertile valley with an abundant food supply. Kupe, the legendary discoverer of New Zealand, is given the credit for finding the Whanganui River, though it was Tamatea, Captain of the Takitimu Canoe, who was the first to fully explore the region. There are plaques along the river commemorating this. Today in Whanganui and along the river you will find many activities for locals and tourists.

After a walk around Wanganui town we drove up to the Botanic gardens. Here you can drive or walk around the gardens, enjoy the lake and birdlife as well as the botanic features. It is situated 11km from town and is open daily from 8.00am till dusk. It has many different garden areas including Native bush sections and wetlands.

As mentioned there is no rest when staying with my brother. After a delicious ice cream in the gardens we were off to the beach. We drove down to Kai Iwi beach, lovely water and  safe swimming.

Time was now getting on so we started to make tracks back to Bulls. We had a big day to prepare for as the following day we were going to Kapiti Island. Well before arriving in New Zealand Peter and Trish had said they would like to take us there so we had made a few enquiries about what to expect.

Kapiti is one of New Zealand's most valuable nature reserves, and it is the only large island sanctuary for birds between the Hauraki Gulf in the north and New Zealand's southern outlying islands. Visitor Access Permits are needed to visit. Ferries have to be booked as private boats are not permitted to land or anchor at the reserve. Visitors can choose from two destinations, Rangatira Point in the middle of the island or the north end.

Kapiti lies about 5 km off the west coast of North Island. It is 10 km long and about 2 km wide. The highest point, Tuteremoana, is 521 m above sea-level. The Island is the summit of a submerged mountain range created by earthquakes 200 million years ago. There are two trails that lead to the top and a lookout from where you can see both the mainland of North Island and the top of South Island. We took the Wilkinson Trail to the top. It is an island of two parts, the wind-blasted hillsides to the west and lush temperate rain forests to the sheltered east.

A lot has been done to make sure human influence is kept to a minimum. Every effort is made to minimise the adverse effects of any introduced plants or animals that have managed to establish on the island. It is a great opportunity to visit such reserves because access to them is so difficult. We had our bags searched before leaving the mainland and had a talk on do's and don'ts while on the island, also about what we might see. The island is now one of the nation's most important sites for bird recovery. Based on counts undertaken from April 1999 to

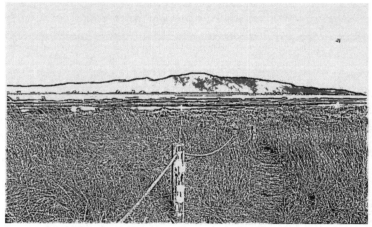

January 2002, species such as kakariki (red-crowned parakeet), robin, bellbird and saddleback, have increased since the eradication of rats. We saw lots of Wekas, a cheeky bird who if you put your rucksack down will try to get into it, as demonstrated by one bird while we were being told about it!

It provides an opportunity for people to observe birds that are either very rare or absent from the mainland. Stitchbird, kokako, takahe, brown teal, and saddleback have all been transferred to Kapiti since the 1980s. Earlier releases (1890s to 1910s) included two forms of brown kiwi and weka. The little spotted kiwi thrives on Kapiti Island but is now extinct on the mainland.

The vegetation is also interesting.  Some of the ancient trees and original forest cover have survived in the deep gullies that you pass as you wind upwards on the path towards the summit. The main forests on the island today are kohekohe, tawa and kanuka. Many parts of the island are covered in scrub dominated by different species of fern. Some plants, such as karo, have been introduced to Kapiti because their flowers provided valuable food for nectar-eating birds.

On the boat trip to and from the island if you are lucky, you can often see gannets, fluttering shearwaters, and little blue penguins. There is an eco toilet on the summit of the island and one at the bottom near the landing point.  We had to take all the food and drink we needed for the day with us. You are left to walk at your own pace, stop to admire the birds and the views and are picked up from the beach later in the day. There were lots of seagulls with nests and young chicks on the beach. Also lots of pieces of Paura shell.

To get to the ferry on time we had to leave at six thirty in the morning as we had over 100  Kilometres to drive to get to Paraparaumu Beach from where the ferry left. This was going to take a couple of hours and we wanted a coffee and snack before leaving on the ferry.

The Department of Conservation issue 50 permits per day to the Nature Reserve on Rangatira Point and 18 permits daily to the North End public land at Waiorua Bay. These have to be booked before you can book a ferry crossing.

Travel Tip : Book as early as possible as permits can be booked up to 3 months in advance. Permits are obtained from Department of Conservation on or email kapiti.island@doc.govt.nz

On our return we went to the Lindale centre for some retail therapy and Waikanae Beach.

Waikanae is surrounded by open farmland and forest with the Tasman Sea on one side and the rugged Tararua Range on the other. Waikanae Beach, the township is a quiet town, popular with families and retired people. Many new cafes have opened up in Waikanae and Waikanae Beach for both the locals and visitors to the Kapiti Coast.

The town and surrounding area is noted for its long beach and wide river mouth, opposite Kapiti Island which lies four kilometres offshore in the Tasman Sea. The waters between Waikanae Beach and Kapiti Island are a marine reserve, and whales are sometimes spotted on their migration routes through this stretch of sea. The beach itself was black sand but is popular for water sports and long walks.

The next morning we were going off to the eastern side of south island, but before we went we had a little look around Bulls (as we hadn't had chance yet)! There is a lovely little museum with historical artefacts and information including memorabilia from the New Zealand Mounted Rifles Brigade. Also it has a great little bookshop (collect-a-bull) what else! There are clothing, food, gift, flower and butchers shops etc etc. In particular on the highway 3 there is Skullys, who make and sell natural body soaps, creams and bath products.

Scullys is well known locally and has been making some of New Zealands finest bath, body and home products since 1992. The unique ranges are inspired by nature and the beautiful New Zealand environment. The products are made for your well being by helping to nourish and replenish the skin using the finest natural essential oils. The smell of perfume as you walk in is wonderful. We bought some lovely gifts in here which were also beautifully gift wrapped at no extra charge.

After one of Peter's special coffees we set off once again. We were going over to the eastern side of the island, crossing the Tararua mountains the highest of which is 1,571 mts or over 5,000ft to us. The idea was to go over the Manawatu Gorge but the road has been closed since a landslip in August and a further slip in October 2011. Although there are alternative routes they are longer and the roads are not built to cope with all the traffic they are currently having to take. Having said that, to us the route still seemed quiet. There are several great views on YouTube of the actual slip and you can appreciate from these how difficult it is to repair the road with so much rock and mud to move and with such steep sides to the gorge.

The Manawatu Gorge (in Maori Te Apiti, meaning 'The Narrow Passage') runs between two mountain ranges, the

Ruahine and Tararua Ranges, linking the west and Hawke's Bay regions. The Manawatu Gorge is significant because, unlike most gorges, the Manawatu River is a water gap, that means it runs directly through the surrounding ranges from one side to the other.

The road through the Gorge, State Highway 3, was completed in 1872. It is the primary link between the two sides of the lower North Island. It is sometimes closed by slips, especially in bad weather. According to the New Zealand Transport Agency, the road will be closed until mid-2012.

A tramping track, the Manawatu Gorge Track, runs parallel to the gorge on the south side through native bush. So instead of this route we took the slow and winding journey over the Pahiatua Track, then Highway 2 to Masterton, following the wine trail through Greytown and Featherston.

Masterton is in the Wairarapa region of New Zealand and is just an hour away from the capital city, Wellington. Here you drive past working farms, country gardens, vineyards and the region's unique natural heritage. The rugged mountains to the west and the untamed Pacific Ocean to the east make it feel quite isolated and remote. People here have always lived off the land and today the region is renowned for its wine and food which makes it a treasure trove for gourmets. The wine the world raves over is the Pinot Noir from the nearby Martinborough Wine Village. "Toast Martinborough", New Zealand's most exclusive wine, food and music event, takes place amongst the vineyards of Martinborough.

Masterton is the largest town in the Wairarapa, a geographical region that is separated from metropolitan Wellington by the mountains. It is a thriving community with an urban population of 19,900. The Wairarapa Line railway, which opened to Masterton on 1st November 1880, allowed many residents easy access to work in the cities of Wellington, Lower Hutt and Upper Hutt. Named after the pioneer Joseph Masters, it was first settled by Europeans in May 1854. Local industries are linked mainly to the surrounding farming community. The town is the headquarters of the annual Golden Shears sheep-shearing competition.

After Masterton we stopped at Paua World in Carterton, where many different products are made from the shells in the factory there. There is also a cafe and picnic area where we had lunch. Carterton is also known for its Daffodil Carnival, a local tradition since 1920 with seven acres of daffodils open to the public for picking.

At the Paua factory you can go inside and see them working on the shells. We had seen bits of Paua shells on the beach at Kapiti and often on the Maori engravings including those at Waitangi. The Paua is actually a small group of shells collectively known as paua but there are some which are unique to New Zealand. These shellfish have been used for food since ancient times and particularly in the diet of coastal Maori. Most countries have their own local names, Abalone (North America), Ormer (Guernsey), Mutton Fish (Australia and early NZ) and Awabi (Japan) being some of the best known.

Paua is the most colourful shell in the world, others have some colour, but are not as brilliant. Paua are marine monovalve molluscs that eat seaweed and live clinging to rocks at depths of 1 - 10 metres. They can be found around most of  New Zealand's rocky shoreline. However, the larger and more important specimens, are found in the cold waters around Stewart Island and Southland. This is where the factory at Carterton get their shells which they use to make jewellery as their colour is more vibrant.

They have holes in their shell for breathing and reproduction. Starfish are the Paua's most formidable predator as they have learnt to suffocate the Paua by putting their tentacles over the breathing holes thus forcing the Paua to let go of the rock.

Sustainable management practices of the paua fisheries are in place in New Zealand including quotas. The largest, most common and best known of the New Zealand species is the Haliotis Iris species. The shellfish is

black and the interior of the shell has cloudy waves of rainbow colours with blues and green being dominant. These shells were used by the Maori to add a gleam of life to the eyes in their carved figures. I now have a beautiful Paua bracelet thanks to Peter and Trish.

After lunch at Carterton we carried on to Greytown. Here was a lovely clean main street with lots of galleries, cafes and antique shops, great for a bit more retail therapy. The town claims to have the most complete main street of Victorian architecture and today its revival is largely based on its architecture. Retailers like the butcher have reversed their 1970s street frontage and reverted to a more Victorian one. It has a great regional history museum, the Cobblestones Museum which is located on Main Street.

Heritage buildings are protected by the Greytown Community Heritage Trust and the Greytown Hotel claims to be one of New Zealand's oldest surviving hotels. Greytown is a popular weekend and holiday destination. We had an interesting walk round here and there is plenty to see for all tastes.

It is also home to the Wairarapa Wine Centre which is managed by an English girl who trained with Majestic wines in England. The wine centre only opened in 2012 and promotes local wine and olive producers. The climate here is quite challenging for wine growing as it has cool southerly winds and therefore small crops. Apparently this means the wines have a unique and intense flavour.

Then to Featherston near the shores of Lake Wairarapa, the largest wetland area in the lower North

Island and a significant nesting ground for native and migratory birds. Apart from antique shops and cafés, this town's key attractions are its museums.

Having spent a long time travelling in the car that day we were ready for a walk and our next stop which was the Kaitoke Regional Park. Although only 45 minutes from Wellington it sits in the foothills of the Tararua Ranges. It has steep hills covered in thick forests of rata, rimu and beech. The Hutton river gorge also flows through it. There are many tracks you can walk along and many safe spots for swimming in the river or in tranquil pools. It is here that the set for Rivendell in the Lord of the Rings Trilogy, was created in a magical part of the forest.

In 1939 the untouched forests of the Kaitoke Regional Park and the Hutton Water Collection Area were purchased to supply water for the Wellington Region. It was identified as a potential Regional Park because of its unspoilt forests. There are many different walking trails from 15 minutes to day walks. We took the Swingbridge Track following the Hutt River downstream through the forest

and going over the swing bridge.

Time was getting on and Peter wanted to show us where they lived when they first moved to New Zealand. So we set off for Belmont, a suburb of Wellington in Lower Hutt. It is on the west bank of the Hutt River, on the Wellington-Hutt main road, and across the river from the centre of Lower Hutt.

It borders the Belmont Regional Park and is surrounded by bush and beautiful views. Many day walks are accessed through the area and it is a popular area for mountain biking with Old Coach Road and Hill Road Track being popular.

We also passed the quarry near Wellington where they had filmed Helms Deep (Lord of the Rings).

Travel Tip: There is a useful book you can buy that gives nearly all of the Lord of the Rings locations if you are interested in these.

We then had quite a drive home back to Bulls of approximately 100 miles. We returned to Highway 1 via the Paekakriki Hill Road. This was the main road north until a road bridge was built at Paremata in 1939. Although a slow and winding road we were rewarded with a lookout as we approached the coast with fantastic views to the north and to Kapiti Island. It was almost nine when we got in, we had a meal to get and Jeff and I had to pack as we needed to leave early next morning for a flight from Wellington to Queenstown. We had another great meal and BBQ coutesy of the family and a long chat giving some thought about where and what we might like to visit when we returned in about ten days time. (I did mention that we had no rest in Bulls)!

It wasn't just that we had to get up early the next day but also had to drive to Te Anau after our flight to Queenstown, and we were expecting a very long outing the following day. We hoped that we had not arranged things a little too tight.

# *Fiordland*

We knew we had to leave two and a half hours to get to the airport as you have to get through Wellington and it would be busy with morning traffic. We left at seven am after a quick coffee and hoped to get breakfast en-route. As it happened though we didn't really see anywhere early on and then got caught in heavy traffic approaching the suburbs of Wellington. We had a really slow journey so decided to wait until we got to the airport for food. Dropped the car off without anything eventful happening and checked in. Check in is all Self Service so we spent a while trying to sort that out, I was trying to scan my e ticket in the wrong place! A very helpful member of New Zealand Airlines helped us – in fact did it for us. All sorted though and bags delivered we found flying internally very laid back, there were not the checks we seem to have and you could take drinks and liquids with you. It was a small plane, an Aerospatiale ATR72 seating 68 people. En route we had good views over Christchurch and along the east coast of south island, followed by the mountain ranges as we neared our destination. We had booked this flight with Air New Zealand and it all went very smoothly.

Air New Zealand began as TEAL (Tasman Empire Airways Limited) in 1940, operating flying boats on trans-Tasman routes. Following World War II, TEAL operated weekly flights from Auckland to Sydney, and then added Wellington and Fiji to its routes. The New Zealand and Australian governments purchased a 50% stake each in TEAL in 1953, and the airline ended flying boat operations and moved to propeller airliners by 1960. In 1965 TEAL became Air New Zealand—the New Zealand government having purchased Australia's 50% stake. It is now based in Auckland and operates scheduled passenger flights to 27 domestic destinations.

Travel Tip: I had been looking at internal flight costs for some time when suddenly cheaper seats were available. I think they must release Smart Saver seats in batches as there were originally none showing as available online and they were substantially cheaper. So persevere and wait to see if they change.

We arrived after a two hour flight into a windy Queenstown , collected the luggage and went to sort out the car hire. Having filled in the paperwork we were just about to go and find the car when Jeff realised  he couldn't find his driving glasses! He thought he may have left them in the car we left in Wellington.  I have to say I wasn't particularly sympathetic having already lost his coat and having twice gone all through our hand luggage!!  Fortunately we were using the same car hire company (Avis) for each separate hire so we went back to the office and they rang back to Wellington where a kind lady went to check the car and duly found them. I would like at this point to formally record my thanks to her but she will probably never know. They arranged to courier them over to Queenstown airport from where we could collect them when we returned two days later.

So we finally found the car and set off for Te Anau. Although sunny the weather forecast was for deteriorating weather and particularly strong winds later that day. The weather for the following day was even worse and that was our big trip to Milford Sound (a bit worrying).

The road from Queenstown starts by heading south and skirting the edge of Lake Wakatipu towards Kingston which features several walking tracks and a golf course. From here the drive is beautiful down to Garston with wide-open views of Southland pastures. We stopped at the Garston Hotel for a coffee and food, of which there was a good choice. There were no other customers inside and it was like stepping into the past but the owner was really chatty and cheerful. He did warn that there was a weather warning out because of the high winds which were getting worse.

The historic Garston Hotel was first established in 1876, but is now an art-deco country hotel set in rural countryside. It is ideally located on the main scenic route to Te Anau. Famed for being New Zealand's most inland hotel and set beside New Zealand's most famous trout fishing river the Mataura.

From Garston the road continues to Five Rivers and then across to Mossburn – the deer capital of New Zealand. After Mossburn, you're now directly on the road to Te Anau. The wind was getting stronger by the minute and you could feel it buffeting the car.

Talk about scenery beyond imagination. The views become so beautiful that the road to Te Anau is a pleasure to drive. Easy, rolling countryside leads to the shores of Lake Te Anau. This is the largest of the South Island's many lakes. On the western side, South Fiord leads into the massive and densely forested Murchison Mountains. Even in murky weather we could see why this is a "must do" tourist destination. After Te Anau, the road then leads you to Milford Sound, a place that exists solely for travellers who come to see Milford Sound, the fiord.

Te Anau itself is on the edge of New Zealand's second-largest lake and is the main visitor base for Fiordland National Park. It is the gateway for walking the Milford, Routeburn or Kepler tracks. It is a beautiful spot with plenty of choice for eating, drinking and accommodation. We had booked ahead as it was the busy season.

We arrived in Te Anau as the rain started to get really heavy, did a quick shop and decided to eat in the room of our motel, which had a well equipped kitchen. We had had a long, tiring day (or few days). We confirmed our trip and had an early night as the next day was due to be a very busy one, but at least we weren't driving.

Before coming to New Zealand we had several discussions on whether to drive to Milford Sound ourselves so we could stop at leisure and do as we wished or to book a trip. We had decided to book a full day out with a company called "Trips and Tramps" which included a nature cruise on Milford Sound and a walk to Key Summit on the way back. They were a company that seemed to offer a personal approach with a relaxed timetable. They have local guides who share their knowledge and passion for the area and give you all the insight into Fiordland and Milford Sound you could wish for. Because they are small groups they don't have to rush and ran what they called a "flexible timetable". This gave us time to enjoy the majestic views and breathe the fresh air.

And so we come to one of the best days ever, the ones you remember when you are back home doing the ironing, the one you remember ALWAYS.

Despite the wind, rain and thunder all night, we managed to get up and have breakfast before being picked up at our hotel at 8am.

The weather forecast had been dreadful, heavy rain and wind and we thought we were going to be unfortunate and not see too much. However the storm seemed to have blown itself out overnight and although cloudy the day was beginning to look a little more hopeful. The trips and tramps minibus picked us up just before eight. The first bonus was that there were only five of us on the trip plus our leader and a young American who was doing some work for them. We consisted of two girls, one from Denmark and one from Holland, a young guy from Switzerland, Jeff and I. We were an eclectic mix and it was interesting finding out where the others had been in New Zealand and about their life at home. We certainly weren't short of conversation! Our guide was particularly interesting. Originally he had been a teacher, then a farmer and had a passion for the outdoors. In the winter when the tours don't run he works for the highways clearing the roads and making sure the road signs are all standing and visible. He remembered one winter having to clean all the lights in the Homer Tunnel! He also checks possum traps down in the Milford area.

So the seven of us set off on our journey down the road to Milford Sound. It is described as one of the most beautiful routes in the world and is a World Heritage Highway. The company we were travelling with also had the contract to deliver the post down the Milford road so it was interesting visiting remote homesteads to deliver or pick up mail and learning about their history and lifestyle.

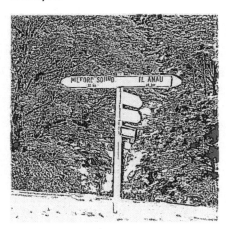

The road to Milford Sound is 119 kilometres and takes about two hours without stops. The first part of the road follows the edge of Lake Te Anau. Lake Te Anau is the largest lake in Fiordland. According to Maori mythology long ago a priest called Te Horo lived in a village in the west. Nearby was a secret, magic spring known only to Te Horo and his wife. The spring was said to be bottomless with pure water and an abundance of fish. On leaving for a journey Te Horo told his wife to tell no-one about the spring. She took a lover and disobeyed him. The water then rose by magic and filled the valley forming Lake Te Anau.

The western side of Lake Te Anau is particularly remote. Boats and float planes provide the only way to visit. The Murchison Mountains over here provide a sanctuary for a rare flightless bird, the Notornis. This was thought to be extinct until it was rediscovered in 1948.

There is a lot of rock debris left from the glacier that gouged out this valley, along with lots of shrubs including manuka (tea tree) and bracken. We stopped at five mile lookout and were introduced to some of the native plants and also Milford's most annoying resident the sandfly.

Travel Tip: take plenty of strong insect repellent for the west coast.

Sandflies are found wherever there is flowing water and bush and only the females bite. The West Coast and Fiordland are infamous for their sandflies. The terminus of the Milford Track, where trampers board the ferry to Milford Sound, is called Sandfly Point. Legend has it that the sand fly was sent to Milford as a curse to stop people from staying forever.

You will rarely be attacked by one sandfly as they seem to hunt in packs. If you manage to see only one then the rest of its friends are probably busy sucking your blood. If you are walking in the bush or kayaking on a river, the sandflies will leave you alone as they cannot keep up. However when you stop for that well earned break or rest, a whole cloud of sandflies will quickly find you. They do not like either wind or rain so bad weather does have some reward.

In the Westland Region, every tour operator and outdoor adventure store will have locally made sandfly repellent. It is a good idea to buy it as the repellent from other places in the world does not work as effectively. The locals have had 100 years to figure out how not to become daily blood donors so you can trust them to concoct an effective solution . DEET is the main active ingredient and is far more effective than the natural products. Covering up can also provide effective protection from swarming sandflies

We then stopped off at Te Anau Downs from where we could see the departure wharf for the Milford Track and our next stop was Mirror Lakes. These lakes provide outstanding reflective views of the Earl Mountains. There is a little boardwalk that you can walk around just here to stretch your legs. The road now starts to enter some of the most striking and staggeringly beautiful scenery . It winds through the forested mountains with constant views of waterfalls, valleys and rivers, all different and all perfect in their own individual ways.  It is a challenging and in places narrow and winding road so we were glad to be driven and just enjoy the scenery and expertise of our guide. There are also no fuel stations along the route! We then came to The Divide from where we were going to walk later in the day. As well as the walk to Key Summit this is also the start of the Routeburn and Greenstone Tracks.

Arriving at the Homer Tunnel the lights were on red so we were able to stop and get some shots of the cheeky Keas that were around the entrance. The driver was not enamoured of them as they peck at the rubber around the windows of the coaches and cause a lot of damage. The kea is an alpine parrot. They are very intelligent and can live up to 29 years.

William Homer and George Barber discovered the Homer saddle in January 1889. Homer thought a tunnel through here would provide access to the Sound. It was eventually completed in 1954. It is 1.2kms long, is downhill all the way and isn't reinforced at all! It is the only access point to Milford and is often closed due to snow or avalanche risk.

After the tunnel the descent into Milford Sound continues dropping 3,000 ft over the next eleven miles through the Cleddau Valley. Here we saw thick native vegetation including conifers such as Rimu, tree ferns and shrubs. Buttercups and daisies were also growing here among the alpine plants. It feels as though coaches and cars shouldn't be there. It was especially atmospheric with the cloud and mist rising and falling, changing the view minute by minute.

The weather had been constantly improving as we got closer and now the clouds were much higher and most of the mountains could be seen. The variations in cloud levels gave a dramatic effect to many of the views. Mount Tutoko at 9,042ft is the highest peak. On a good day you see it just before reaching the Sound. However it is Mitre Peak that inspires you even though it's only 5,560ft, as you reach your destination.

We arrived at the Sound around 10.45 for an 11am cruise. Once there, other than the boats for the trip,s there is a cafe and a lodge and that's it. It is very remote with only the one road in. Milford Sound is a place that exists solely as an embarkation point for travellers who come to see Milford Sound, the fiord. Milford Sound is named after Milford Haven in Wales, and the Cleddau River which flows into the sound is also named after its Welsh namesake. The Māori named the sound Piopiotahi after the thrush-like Piopio bird which is now extinct.

We had been advised by our guide which side of the boat to sit for the best views etc but none of that really mattered because we had a 68 seater boat and just 12 passengers on board. There was lots of space inside and out, a bar with food and drinks and complimentary tea and coffee for the whole journey. We had booked the nature cruise so had a skipper, the food manager and a specialist nature guide for just a very small group so it felt particularly personal. Throughout the cruise the guide shared stories about the history of the fiord and was also happy to answer any questions. With the weather also now as near as it gets to perfect down there we wondered what we had done to deserve such a great outing. Apparently it rains over 200 days each year and there is an average annual rainfall of over 6,000ml.

The cruise has a flexible itinerary so we just moved along looking at different wildlife and spectacles as we saw them. Milford Sound is home to a permanent colony of New Zealand fur seals and we saw many of them sleeping on the rocks. Also we saw one catching a fish and thrashing it in the water to kill it. We also got close-up experiences of Milford Sound's rainforests, soaring rock walls and spectacular waterfalls. After the heavy overnight rain these seemed particularly impressive. We got so close to some of the waterfalls that water soaked the foredeck. The mountains seem to stretch tall, straight up from the sea and thick rainforest was clinging to the precipitous rock walls. The waterfalls are particularly magnificent as they tumble hundreds of metres to the sea below.

Lady Bowen and Stirling Falls are Milford's two permanent waterfalls pumping water into the sea all year but there are many others that keep flowing on an almost constant basis due to the wet weather there. Lady Bowen Falls is the first waterfall you see after you start your cruise. It is 162 metres high, named after Diamantina Bowen who was the wife of George Bowen, the fifth

Governor of New Zealand. The falls actually generate electricity for the Milford village.

Looking back towards Milford Sound village, you see it sitting at sea level at the base of the Sheerdown Range of mountains, whose highest peak is 1871 metres (6139 feet). This range gets its name from the steepness of its slopes, something shared with most of the mountains surrounding the fjords.

The sounds or fiords wind their way between the lofty mountains. There are actually twelve sounds, three of which are particularly well known. Doubtful Sound is known for its link with Lake Manapouri, the road over the Wilmot Pass and the Hydro Station. Dusky Sound was written about by Captain Cook and after his first visit here it became the most popular anchorage in New Zealand. Milford Sound because it's beauty has attracted millions of tourists over the years.

A surprising aspect of the fjord's wildlife is the presence of red corals and black corals on the flooded walls. However, the huge volume of fresh water flowing into the fjord from the surrounding forests produces a 10 or 20 meter thick layer of fresh water on top of the salt water. The fresh water is stained dark brown from the tannin in the leaves, which cuts down the light levels in the salt water below, allowing the coral to grow at shallower depths. There is also an underwater observatory near to the village to allow visitors to see the coral and some of the other marine life.

As we got nearer to the Tasman Sea the cloud level dropped and the sea got rougher, the Sound took on a different atmosphere, no less spectacular just different but on re-entering the Sound the sun was out again. Whatever the fiord's mood, brooding and wet, or serene in the sunshine – it can't fail to inspire you. Mitre Peak, the Lion, Mt Pembroke and the Bowen Falls all reflect their striking profiles in the waters of Milford Sound. However it is the silence of Milford Sound that I will remember, the fresh air and the pure water. These are things that money cannot buy.

As we returned to Milford we couldn't believe the queues for the lunchtime cruises! We found our guide and returned to the minibus for the second part of the trip.

Possible travel tip!: book an early cruise as the coaches from Queenstown arrive later and the lunchtime ones are therefore busier.

Walking, or as they say in New Zealand 'tramping', was to follow. We had a choice of ascending up the Routeburn Track to Key Summit through rainforest and into the alpine environment  or alternatively we could explore the secluded lower Hollyford Valley with the nature guide. Once up on the summit you get panoramic views of the surrounding Fiordland Mountains. We had left this decision until the day as we were not sure what the weather would be like and the Summit seemed a good choice for a clear day and the valley if the weather was inclement. All five of us wanted to do Key Summit though. Our friend from Switzerland had recently completed the Routeburn Track but the weather had been poor so he had not gone up to the summit top. Up until that particular day we had always thought of ourselves as fairly quick walkers but we found ourselves bringing up the rear with these fit youngsters. We all got to the top though and were met by our guide who caught us up having set off later! He then provided us with a

wilderness tea break with home style biscuits and billy tea.

On the top is an Alpine Nature Walk. It is a thirty minute loop track passing alpine tarns and presenting spectacular views. There are panels as you go round giving information about the area.

Key Summit was so named because it is the key to the origin of the three major river systems of Southland and Otago, the Hollyford River flows to the west coast, the Eglinton-Waiau Rivers flow to the south coast and the Greenstone-Clutha Rivers flow to the east coast. The three river valleys are all visible from Key Summit.

South west New Zealand is one of the great wilderness areas of the southern hemisphere. It is known to the Maori as Te Wahipounami ( the place of greenstone). Early Maori would have travelled through this area in search of pounami. The first Europeans came in search of routes to the west coast, land for pasture and later gold.

Returning back down the trail to the minibus we continued back up the Milford Road to Te Anau. We were all feeling pleasantly weary and contemplating what a fabulous day it had been. We felt privileged to have seen such spectacular and awe inspiring sights. Needless to say we slept well that night.

Travel Tip: double check the fuel gauge before departing Te Anau.

# *The West Coast*

The next day we were due to move on to Queenstown. We spent the morning having a look around Te Anau and went to the cinema to see the renowned film Shadowlands, Ata Whenua. It takes you on an exhilarating journey through the awe inspiring landscape of Firodland. It is an outstanding film but doesn't really compare with the real experience in my opinion. We wished we could have stayed another night in Te Anau so that we could have taken the ferry over the Lake to Brod Bay and walked part of the Kepler Track back to town.

Instead we drove to Manapouri. Manapouri itself is on the eastern shore of Lake Manapouri. It is the gateway to both Doubtful Sound and Dusky Sound and the starting point for lots of local walking tracks. It is popular with tourists, particularly during the summer months. Lake Manapouri has one hundred miles of shoreline but only two of these are skirted by road. With the building of the huge underground hydro station on the Western Arm of the lake, life changed here. A village was built to house the construction workers, motels arrived and roads were sealed. Most of the electricity generated at the power station serves the Tiwai Point Aluminium Smelter. Here again were spectacular views across the Lake which we left to continue on to Queenstown.

Just before reaching our destination though we needed to call in at the airport if you remember. I circled the car park looking for a space and Jeff went to the car hire desk. Just as promised his driving glasses had been delivered and were waiting for him. All this for just 20 dollars!! (A lot cheaper than a new pair of glasses though).

So on to our arrival in Queenstown, the adrenalin capital of New Zealand! What has Queenstown got to offer the tourist? Here are just some of the activities available. You can also do virtually any combination of them for a set price. If this is your sort of fun then you need to spend some time here - and money!

1. Canyon Swing
2. Jet boat Safaris
3. Skydive
4. Kayaking
5. White water Rafting
6. Ski Packages
7. Bungy jumping
8 Rock Climbing & Abseiling
9. Aerobatic Stunt Plane - Aerostunts
10. Via Ferrata
11 Canyoning
12 Clay Target Shooting

13 Fly Fishing
14 Hang Gliding
15 Heli Skiing
16 Horse Riding
17 Hot Air Balloons
18 Kayaking
19 Lake Fishing
20 Mountain Biking
21 Paragliding
22 Quad biking
23 Rafting
24 River Boarding
25 River Surfing
26 Segway
27 Ski Guiding
28 Snowshoeing - Guided Nature Walks
29 The Luge
30 Ziptrek
31 G Force Tandem Paragliding

Travel Tip : There are other attractions in Queenstown that don't involve thrills and spills.

The place we were staying  was the Goldridge resort just outside Queenstown. The rooms had large patio doors looking out over Lake Wakatipu and onto The Remarkables. It was a stunning view. The restaurant had the same views so breakfast and dinner were spectacular affairs and you could eat outside on the balcony if you desired. The staff were very friendly and helped arrange our next accommodation for us. We had looked at several possibilities for the next leg of our journey and they booked it for us.

So what should we do while here apart from enjoying the fabulous view from our room over the lake and mountains. We had contemplated horse riding which we had both enjoyed in Canada but we decided to buck the trend here and do something that wasn't going to give either of us a heart attack.

We drove north to Arrowtown. Arrowtown is a historic village twenty minutes from Queenstown passing the beautiful Lake Hayes and the bungy jumping on the way. It was originally known as "Fox"s", and then "the township of Arrow". It was gold that brought thousands of miners to the Arrow River in 1861 when it was one of the world's richest sources of alluvial gold.

Jack Tewa, a shearer, was the first to discover gold around May 1861, followed by others in 1862. Although there were attempts to keep the discovery secret, this didn't happen and there were 1,500 miners camped down on the Arrow River by the end of 1862. Twelve thousand ounces (340 kgs) of gold were carried out on the first gold escort in January 1863.

Gold eventually became harder to extract and the European miners headed to the west coast for the riches there. The Otago Provincial Government then invited Chinese miners to come to the Otago goldfields. The Chinese created a separate settlement in Arrowtown, remaining until 1928. It is really interesting to visit as you can still walk round the old Chinese village and go inside reconstructed houses and stores. There is a lot of history about the Chinese and other gold miners in the Arrowtown Museum which is informative and very good value for money.

After the initial gold rush, a more permanent town began to establish itself. Avenues of trees were planted in 1867 in an attempt to make Arrowtown look more like the European towns the settlers had left behind.

Fire was always a threat because of the wooden buildings. A large fire in December 1896 resulted in the destruction of the Morning Star Hotel, Campbell's bakery and the top storey of Pritchard's Store. In spite of fires and through careful preservation, Arrowtown still has around 70 buildings, monuments and features remaining from the gold rush era. The legacy is unique in that now the buildings have a new lease of life with trendy shops, galleries, cafes etc occupying them. It is a pleasure to look round mixing the old with the new and finding shops with goods you don't see anywhere else.

By the turn of the 21st Century Arrowtown had become a popular visitor destination and one of the fastest growing towns in New Zealand. It's spectacular scenery attracts visitors from around the world.

It is now a living but significant holiday destination. There are small historic cottages, shops with tiny windows and uneven floors, instead of becoming a ghost town it is a thriving tourist centre.

Spectacular scenery, four very distinct seasons and a tranquil atmosphere attract visitors from New Zealand and around the world. Gold panning, touring the authentic buildings, going to the cinema, walking the nearby trails are just some of the activities available to take part in while there. It is renowned for its extensive range of history and recreational walking tracks which range from 30 minutes to up to three days. Maps of the tracks can be obtained from the Arrowtown Museum.

Arrowtown now has a population of 2,400 who share their village atmosphere with visitors. Services include a medical centre, schools, post office and pharmacy. Nearby are an international airport, hospital, ski areas, ice and curling rinks, sports, events and aquatic centres.

We spent most of the day here and then felt obliged to go into Queenstown itself to have a look round. After struggling to park (the only time this actually happened in New Zealand), we walked down to the waterfront.

Here there is a vibrant, cosmopolitan community and the waterfront was buzzing. The towering peaks of the Remarkables Ranges dominate the landscape, dwarfing the town as it stretches along the waters of Lake Wakatipu. Wakatipu, at 82km long is the third largest lake in the country and provides a stunning, panoramic outlook for all the bars, hotels and restaurants that cluster along the shore. As we wandered through the town there was live music playing, stalls selling local goods and food, giving it a carefree holiday atmosphere.

The waterfront face of Queenstown today hides a rich pioneering history, with links to gold, farming and of course the Lady of the Lake, the TSS Earnslaw, launched on the lake in 1912 and one of the few coal-fired passenger-carrying vessels still operating in the southern hemisphere.

Despite all this, the nobility of the mountains, the broad blue waters of the lake and clear, sharp air are what we will remember of this unique town.

Our journey the next morning was a long one. We had 487 kilometres to drive which is approximately six hours driving time, but we knew it would mean the whole day for us as we like to stop off and look at places we pass through or do short walks to waterfalls and lakes. We were driving north to Hokitika on the west coast. We

started the journey slowly as we decided to go over the Crown range of mountains rather than Highway 6. This road winds up through the mountains with great views. There is a little town called Cadrona about half way to Wanaka which is already in the ski area but is currently being developed.

The town though is like walking into the past. It nestles in the hills of the Cardrona Valley and The Cardrona Hotel which was established in 1863, is one of New Zealand's oldest hotels but offers both quality accommodation and traditional hospitality having had major refurbishment. It is full of history from the gold rush era. It is also close to 5 major ski areas.

We continued on to Wanaka. In a way this seemed like a small version of Queenstown, beautiful scenery, lots of sports, but more tranquil. Lake Wanaka calls itself a Lifestyle Reserve. This means it combines it's spectacular scenery with a genuine sense of community. The operators there are impassioned about their way of life and want to share this. Lake Wanaka's spectacular location at the foot of the Southern Alps with the wilderness of the Mt Aspiring National Park nearby makes it a magnet for people who love the outdoors. It's values are supported by the   New Zealand Tourism Strategy 2015 which refers to Manaakitanga and Kaitiakitanga :

Manaakitanga implies a reciprocal responsibility upon a host, and an invitation to a visitor to experience the very best they have to offer.

Kaitiakitanga is about guardianship, care and protection. It provides a basis for their approach to sustainably managing their natural, cultural, and built environment for current and future generations.

From Wanaka we travelled north along Lake Hawea and then continued along the northern part of Lake Wanaka. This was followed by the Haast Pass where we stopped at Thunder Creek Falls. The Haast river flows alongside the South Island's Highway 6. Rain and melt waters feed the river and provide the fuel that drives various waterfalls and rapids along its course .One of these is Thunder Creek falls, located 55 km east of Haast with roadside parking for a few cars. A small track takes you on a short and easy two-minute walk through silver beech forest to a viewing platform opposite where the falls tower over the river. Here the water falls 28 m or so onto a rocky hollow adjoining the river itself. The ferocity of the waterfall depends on recent weather conditions. Fortunately this area rarely has dry periods so you're pretty much guaranteed a good photo opportunity.

After Haast we continued up the west coast past Lake Moeraki and Lake Paringa  to Fox Glacier and Franz Josef.

We had not included a visit to the glaciers on this trip as we just couldn't fit everything in. We had been walking on the glaciers on the Icefields Parkway in Canada so felt this was a place that we would save for a possible return visit. Fox Glacier itself has a real village atmosphere with a great outlook and plenty of food outlets for passing travellers.

One of the must do opportunities here is to drive five minutes west to Lake Matheson a photographers heaven. The waters of the lake reflect a mirror image of some of New Zealand's highest peaks, Aoraki (Mt Cook) and Mt Tasman. There is also a track that circles the lake through native rainforest. It takes approximately one hour to walk this. A further drive from Lake Matheson brings you to Gillespies Beach which is a historic gold mining settlement.

Just twenty five kilometres north of Fox Glacier is Franz Josef. This is a little village of approximately 330 inhabitants five kilometres away from the face of the glacier. It has a number of shops, restaurants and accommodation options.

The glacier area is one of the main tourist attractions of the West Coast, with around 250,000 visitors a year, and up to 2,700 per day. Guided and unguided walks up to and onto the glacier are possible as are helicopter tours.

Apparently the glacial landscape changes almost daily, and some walks include passages through ice tunnels, they are considered quite safe but somewhat strenuous.

We were unable to stay long in the area as we still had around 135 kilometres to drive. The road moved inland as it wound its way round river inlets and it was towards the end of the day when we arrived at our destination Hokitika. We had booked a one night stop here at a small bed and breakfast. Our host had lots of information about the town and places to see even on such a short visit. He obviously loved the town and shared his passion with enthusiasm. Just driving through on the main highway you would think Hokitika had little to offer but in fact it is a thriving place with many visitor attractions based on its historical and natural resources.

The Hokitika" Wildfoods Festival" in early March each year is an extravaganza of gourmet food, based on The

West Coast's natural food sources. The emphasis is on novel, tasty and healthy wildfood. This event regularly attracts 15,000 visitors.

There are also plenty of other regular events such as the annual "take a seat" competition, where designs are invited and the winner gets a grant to create and put up the seat in the town. We took photographs of several of them. It is interesting to look for these unusual and creative seats as you walk around the town. We also arrived shortly after the driftwood and sand sculpture competition and there were still lots of driftwood sculptures to see and photograph along the beach. It was ideal for this as like many of the beaches we had seen it was full of driftwood. It also has a heritage trail, it's own sunset point and a glow worm dell with free viewing of the glow worm colonies. They seem to work hard at organising events to promote the town as there is also the Sand Dune Classic, (a fun day of golf on the beach) and the Kumara Race Day (a day at the races event held in January each year).

After a wander and a very pleasant meal in town we did some window shopping and found the Hokitika Craft Gallery. This was still open and is a co-operative of about fifteen crafts people and artists. Run by its members it sells wood, jade, bone, pottery, fibre and art creations. We found some lovely souvenirs there to take home knowing that they had been made in New Zealand and with lots of information about both the products and the artists.

Travel Tip : Hokitika is a good place for authentic New Zealand souvenirs.

Having driven so far that day we had left ourselves with a much shorter drive the following day. We were beginning to manage the full breakfasts now, our fellow breakfast guests being from Israel on this occasion. They were travelling the opposite way to us, working their way down the coast to Queenstown so we exchanged notes. After this we set off for the Pancake rocks at Punakaiki, north of Greymouth. As we travelled up the coast we kept stopping as there were the most wonderful raw, deserted, wild beaches, the sort that I adore with great names like "perfect strangers beach". Just the name makes me want to go back! All the tourist books and people we had met said we should visit Pancake Rocks, so we did. It reminded me very much of Lulworth Cove in Dorset. It was absolutely packed here, a very popular and busy tourist destination.

Punakaiki is a small community on the edge of the Paparoa National Park and The Pancake Rocks are at Dolomite Point south of the main village. It is a heavily eroded limestone area where the sea bursts though a number of vertical blowholes during high tides. They are known as "pancake rocks" because of the 'pancake'-layering of the limestone and they form the main attraction of the area.

You can walk round and explore them by a number of walkways winding through the rock formations, parts of these are wheelchair-accessible and others are carved stairways up and down the rock faces. It was interesting but very much a set routine with everyone being herded round the same way. Having said that, we did get some spectacular photographs.

We then carried on to Westport and from here we drove through the mountains towards Nelson. There were lots of single lane bridges and great views down valleys and along rivers. It had been a feature of driving over there, these single lane bridges with varying rights of way. I think the most hairy of these was the single lane bridge that was also a railway line, so you had to look out for trains and cars coming at you, they don't have gates on the railway crossings either, just signs telling you to look out for trains. There was fabulous scenery all the way through here. We found a picnic area in the Buller Gorge to stop for a bite to eat and drink.

The Buller Gorge is a deep canyon through which the Buller River flows between Murchison and Westport. It has two sections for the gorge, Upper Buller Gorge and Lower Buller Gorge. The road runs alongside this and also the Stillwater - Westport Line railway.

# *Abel Tasman Coast*

After days of travelling through densely forested areas and seeing little traffic it was very different approaching Nelson. We passed through Richmond where there were several lanes of traffic, very industrial and built up, it even had traffic lights! More by chance and instinct rather than skill we found our accommodation, The Honest Lawyer Pub. It is situated on Nelson's Monaco Peninsula and describes itself as an "Olde Worlde English Country Pub and Hotel". We were staying three nights here so were looking forward not to be living out of the suitcase. In fact we actually unpacked. We stayed in Rose Cottage so had lots of space.

Monaco is one of Nelson's loveliest little suburbs, with its seaside setting but it is also close to the airport. We didn't find this a problem though and had chosen it first because we wanted to explore the Abel Tasman National Park from here and it was the right side of Nelson for that and also it had been recommended by our daughter and son in law who had stayed there on a visit to New Zealand for their honeymoon several years before. We weren't staying in the honeymoon suite though!

What we hadn't been told when we booked it was that the next day was Waitangi Day (6th Feb), and they were shut for the day so we could not get any breakfast or dinner there. This meant we had to go out and do a quick shop so we could get our own breakfast the next morning.

We had heard and read great things about the beaches north from here and the Abel Tasman coast track. It turned out to be one of the highlights of the trip with its stunning scenery and seclusion. We were rewarded with fabulous weather while we were there too.

Abel Tasman National Park is New Zealand's smallest. It protects some of the most natural stretches of easily accessible coastline in New Zealand. The world famous Coast Track enables you to visit the park's private estuaries, golden sand beaches and forested headlands. The park was founded in 1942, and is named after Abel Tasman, who in 1642 became the first European explorer to sight New Zealand.

The strip of coast that is within the boundary of the park is highly distinctive. Granite and marble formations fringe the headlands and the area is covered with native forest. White sandy beaches fill the spaces between trees and tide line inviting you to go down there and explore. The streams that tumble down mossy valleys are crystal clear.

The Abel Tasman Coast Track is a popular tramping track which follows the coastline but there ia also an inland route, the Abel Tasman Inland Track ,which is less frequented. Kayaking, camping and sightseeing are other popular activities in the park. It has a mild climate and high sunshine hours making it popular at any time of year. The Department of Conservation looks after the park and maintains the huts, campsites and tracks there.

There are several water taxi operators which enable day visitors to take advantage of walking sections of the track and be picked up at further landing points later in the day. These run on fixed timetables and you can book between any two points. This is what we planned to do. Canoes can also be hired which was another popular way of exploring the coast.

We set off north on Highway 60 to the nearest large town Motueka. Motueka (meaning 'island of bush with Weka') is known for its great climate and is one of the best areas in the South Island to grow the prized kumara, or maori sweet potato. Tobacco and hops were popular here until the 1980's when apple and kiwifruit orchards and more recently vineyards took over. We passed many of these en route.

Motueka township is a vibrant, friendly and cosmopolitan town. Apparently the long summer days and mild winters attract many people to the town and a large number then choose to stay and call Motueka home. It is the third largest town in the Nelson Province.

Motueka has all the ammenities you would expect in a larger town, with supermarkets, a wide variety of shops and services, artizans, amazing cafes and the Motueka i-Site Visitor Centre. It was here we got all the information we needed for walking on the track and booking the boat.

Leaving here we continued to Kaiteriteri. Kaiteriteri Beach is one of the many magnificent beaches in New Zealand. It is a busy holiday destination for New Zealanders and visitors alike. There are motor camps, backpackers, motel and bed and breakfast accommodation available, along with a general store and fuel. It is from here that many boat and kayak trips leave for the Abel Tasman National Park. We booked a water taxi to take us to Anchorage. On the way we stopped at other beaches for people to disembark and we passed by Split Apple Rock. This interesting rock formation looks exactly as the name suggests, as it rises from the water of Tasman Bay. It is a giant boulder that has been broken in two pieces so cleanly that it looks almost as if a giant hit it with an axe.

As we didn't know how long to leave for our pick up we decided to be collected from the same place later in the day and do a circular walk from here. Anchorage is a beautiful semi-circular bay. We took the walking track leading up to Pitt Head where an ancient Maori pa (fort) site exists. Terracing and food pits are still visible, and you can see why the location was chosen as a defensive site. The views are incredible. Then we walked to Te Pukatea Bay which is a perfect crescent of golden sand and where we relaxed for a while before walking back to Anchorage where the taxi picked us up later in the day. The views up and down this coast are really special. Native wildlife is all around and an essential part of the area. You can hear Tui and bellbirds while watching the cormorants and gannets diving in the clear waters. We also watched boats in the bay and the kayaks which as mentioned were a popular way of exploring the area.

<u>Travel Tip</u>: Use the water taxis to explore these remote beaches, or just do the round trip.

We decided that night to have our own picnic overlooking the estuary as our bar was shut that evening. It had been one of those special days again, so much so that we decided to go back up the coast the following day.

There are two roads to Motueka, the faster one and the scenic one. We took the scenic route the second day by Mapua and Ruby Bay. There are lots of galleries and wine tasting cafes around here and it is a much quieter road. We took advantage of this and an early start to stop off at a couple of the galleries – it was a bit early for the wine!

Instead of going to Kaiteriteri today we continued north to Marahau the southern end of the coastal track. The road to the village passes charming rural farms, forests, lush native bush and lots of birdlife. It is a community of farmers, artisans and tourism operators.

Marahau Village is a much quieter place, a paradise again but without all the commercial trappings or crowds. The beaches line the shore road giving it a tranquil, carefree feeling. The beach offers safe swimming with sheltered waters for most of the year. There is a wonderful cafe there and we had coffee looking out across the beach and sea. The only other tourist building is the information centre for booking taxis and canoes, so REALLY quiet.

As the gateway to the National Park, Marahau is a comfortable and peaceful base and one we would love to stay at in the future. We parked in Marahau and started along the track which firstly crossed the estuary of the Marahau River on the causeway. It then comes to Tinline bay which we went down to and had totally to ourselves. We continued on to Coquilles Bay where we stayed for most of the day. There were very few people about and we went swimming in the fantastically clear water and dried off on the large pieces of driftwood on the beach. The only sounds were the seagulls and and boats passing. It must have been as near to heaven as you can get. You could sit there for hours contemplating life and reflecting on how lucky you were to be there. We met lots of people on the actual track but also there were many little bays that you can access that are either empty or with just a couple of people.

We returned back along the track to the car.

What we wanted to do now was to call at one of the wineries to do some wine tasting before going back to Nelson. After all you can't really go to New Zealand and not do this. We had been trying lots of wine both in restaurants and from supermarkets and made a point of always trying the NZ wines while we were there.

We drove to the Waimea Estate and called at the Cafe in the Vineyard. Here they served food, teas and coffees as well as wine tasting. It was only ten dollars to try three wines and you didn't pay at all if you bought any wine from them. There were full tasting notes and we tried several between us. We bought a few bottles, some for us and some to take for Peter and Trish later in the holiday. We finished off with a long coffee. The Winery Café and Cellar Door is open seven days a week from 10am to 5pm.

Waimea is a family business which started with orchards on the Waimea Plains in the early nineties. They diversified from apples into grape growing and winemaking between 1993 and 1995. The first wine from these vines was produced in 1997 and was an immediate success. In 2006, the last of the apples were pulled out and now they concentrate on wine only.

One of the distinguishing features of Nelson wineries today is that nearly all of them are family owned and Waimea Estates is no exception.

Travel Tip: Be sure to try the wine tasting in one of the many vinyards in the area. They are not expensive and some are free!

So we near the end of our visit to South Island. The following morning we had the relatively short journey to Picton for one night and then were catching the ferry to Wellington.

The city of Nelson is home to a fascinating community of beach, bush and art lovers. We didn't really get to see the city as we spent our time there exploring the beaches of Abel Tasman Park. All we saw of the actual town was as we drove through it on the way to Picton. After Nelson we passed Pelorus  Bridge Scenic Reserve and nearby Canvastown, a place to explore old gold mining fields where thousands tried to get rich  in the 1860s.

We stopped in Havelock, which is known as the Green Shell Mussel Capital of the World. Less than 600 people live in Havelock and it possesses a character all of its own. We had a coffee and a walk around the harbour area which was full of interesting boats and yachts before moving on. This authentic and historic little fishing port is the ideal introduction to the stunning Marlborough Sounds we were heading towards..

# *Picton to Wellington*

Before long we arrived at the picturesque seaside town of Picton, the gateway to the marine, forest and island attractions of the Marlborough Sounds. There are museums  and interesting walks to keep all ages entertained while you're here. This is the starting point for lots of trips into the Sound and for walking all or part of the Queen Charlotte track.

The Marlborough Sounds are made up of an extensive network of sea-drowned valleys created by a combination of land subsidence and rising sea levels. Their coastline is so extensive it amounts to one fifth of New Zealand's total coasts.  According to Māori mythology, the sounds are the prows of the sunken waka (canoe) of Aoraki.

They are made up of steep, wooded hills and small quiet bays. The population is sparse here as access is difficult. Many of the small settlements and isolated houses are only accessible by boat. The main sounds, other than Queen Charlotte Sound, are Pelorus Sound and Kenepuru Sound. Captain Cook visited the sounds in the 1770s, discovering a plant (Cooks Scurvy Grass) high in vitamin C which helped to cure scurvy amongst his crew.

Again we had found a superb little bed and breakfast near the harbour. It was immaculately clean and had views to die for. The owner had lots of information for us and suggestions of things to do before we left. There was tea, coffee, biscuits, wine etc all available in a residents lounge plus wi- fi. Our host suggested we drove out to Karaka Point to get the views over the Sound as it was a lovely sunny day. The Point is eight kilometres by road east of Picton on the far side of Waikawa Bay. A short winding track takes you along the point to a grassed look out. Midway along the track you will see the ramparts and pits of what was a sizeable Maori settlement. It is not known what happened to the occupants but it is thought that they were eventually driven out by Te Rauparaha. There is a large, interesting Maori totem pole here providing great photographic opportunities with the sound in the background..

Back in Picton we then went to the Edwin Fox Museum. The Edwin Fox is the world's 9th oldest ship. She is made of timber and had a varied life.

On her maiden voyage to London via the Cape of Good Hope she carried 10 passengers and a general cargo. She also served the British Government in the Crimean War, reputedly carrying such illustrious passengers as Florence Nightingale. The Edwin Fox then spent a period trading between various Eastern cities carrying coolies from China to Cuba where they were destined to work in the cane fields.

Between 1858 and 1872 Edwin Fox was used primarily for 2 purposes: to sail between England and the East as a trader, including several trips to India carrying a pale ale earning her the nickname of "Booze Barge", and as a troop ship again, making several voyages with troops from the UK. By the 1880's the age of steam had arrived and the sheep industry in New Zealand was booming.

Edwin Fox was fitted out as a floating freezer hulk and was used as such in several South Island ports. She was finally towed to Picton arriving in 1897 where she has remained ever since, initially as a freezer ship, later as a coal hulk and now preserved under cover as a prominent tourist attraction.

The museum is very varied with films, artefacts, letters etc and you can actually go into the ship itself which is really remarkable. The light inside the ship is fantastic for photographs. There was so much to see and time was getting on that we asked if we could come back the next morning using the same tickets which they were happy to let us do

The following morning we sat in bed having a cup of tea and admiring the view over the harbour as a cruise ship slowly wound its way down the Sound and moored in Picton. It was the sort of view that money can't buy. The

Sound must be very deep to allow Cruise ships access. This also meant that Picton itself would be quite busy that day.

Picton foreshore has a small beach connected to the town with lots of attractions like the Sea Horse World Aquarium, a great local aquarium with the representative marine life of the Marlborough Sounds. When we were looking round there was also a small market around that area selling mainly New Zealand items which was interesting. The Inter Islander and other Ferries to the North Island go from here. Along this area there is a wealth of cafe's, pubs and restaurants. There is a shopping street with many galleries and shops with local crafts and gifts as well as the hardware shops, supermarkets etc.

Travel Tip: Picton has a lot to offer including trips to Blenheim so is worth an extra night if at all possible.

Blenheim is named after the Battle of Blenheim (1704), where troops led by John Churchill, 1st Duke of Marlborough defeated a combined French and Bavarian force.

It is the focal point for the Marlborough wine growing region. A number of wineries are located on the towns edges, with many more just a short drive away.

Blenheim is known internationally for its distinctive Sauvignon Blanc and is New Zealand's largest winemaking region with around 65 wineries and 290 grape growers. The main grapes planted are Sauvignon Blanc, Chardonnay, Riesling, Pinot Noir, Pinot Gris and Gewurztraminer.

Our ferry was not until lunchtime so we had plenty of time to look round and go back to the museum. The car drop is at the ferry terminal so that was easy and check in including our suitcases was also very slick and straightforward. We had treated ourselves to an upgrade on the ferry to the first class lounge. We did this mainly as lunch was included so that we only needed to get a light snack that night in Wellington as it would be late afternoon before we arrived. There was lots of space in the lounge and large picture windows. They had lots of New Zealand wines we could try as we were no longer driving! As well as lunch they also later on the journey served afternoon tea with cakes and scones and cream so we felt it had been well worthwhile to pay the extra. The ferry itself though was far from full and there seemed to be lots of room and seats on all the decks.

The journey out of the Sound is great for taking photographs, with lots of inlets and beaches and then into the Cook Strait. The Marlborough Sounds are connected to the Cook Strait at the north-east extreme. At this point, the North Island is at its closest to the South Island, and the inter-island road, rail, and passenger ferry service between Picton and Wellington travels through the sounds.

The main channels of the Marlborough Sounds have calm water and are popular for sailing. Cook Strait, however, is infamous for its strong currents and rough waters, especially when the wind is from the south or north.

The most notable shipwreck in the sounds is that of the Russian cruise liner Mikhail Lermontov, which sank in 1986 in Port Gore, close to the mouth of Queen Charlotte Sound, after striking rocks. One life was lost in the incident. The ship is now a popular dive wreck.

Luckily it was a sunny peaceful day when we travelled so it was a smooth crossing. The 92km voyage takes 3 hours and has been described as "one of the most beautiful ferry rides in the world". I think we would agree with that.

Arriving in Wellington we went straight to our hotel, The Abel Tasman on Willis Street. It was only a short walk from here to all the major attractions such as The Terrace, Courtenay Place, the Michael Fowler Centre, the TSB Arena, Lambton Quay, Te Papa Museum, Wellington's Waterfront and Civic Centre. It was also only a few minutes drive from the Ferry terminal and near to the

Avis office for our hire car. It is a small hotel with few facilities but the rooms were quite spacious and the restaurant lovely in the evenings with plenty of atmosphere. It certainly suited our needs, just a fairly quiet hotel in a quiet area, yet close to the visitor attractions.

After settling in we walked down to the waterfront to get our bearings and also visited the Te Papa Museum which was open late. Te Papa is New Zealand's national museum, renowned for being bicultural, scholarly, innovative, and fun. Their success is built on their relationships with and ability to represent their community.

The collections here span five areas: Art, History, Pacific, Māori, and Natural Environment. A lot of exhibitions are interactive, and there were many different events and education programmes on when we were there. They have a diverse range of Maori material including ancestral carvings, personal ornaments, garments, and weapons. Included in the collection is contemporary Maori visual culture that reflects current ideas about cultural identity, continuity, and change.

It was fascinating and we could have spent hours in there but had to limit our visit to the one evening.

We had one full day in Wellington so the next morning we set off for Lambton Quay, which is not by the sea but a shopping street well back from the waterfront. It used to be known as "Beach Street" and is now in the centre of the business district. As the name implies it was once the foreshore of the original settlement of 1840 that grew into Wellington. The Wairarapa earthquake in 1855 caused the land to lift and has left the street 250 metres from the shoreline.

Lambton Quay is named after John Lambton, 1st Earl of Durham, the first chairman of directors of the New Zealand Company.

Lambton Quay and Willis Street together form what is known locally as the Golden Mile and is a major commercial area along with Cuba Street and Manners Street.

The Wellington Cable Car runs from Lambton Quay to the top of the Botanic Garden and it was this we were heading for.

The Cable Car is one of Wellington's oldest and most popular tourist attractions. Within 5 minutes  the cable car whisks you past Kelburn Park and Victoria University to the top entrance of the Wellington Botanic Gardens where there is a magnificent lookout over the City and harbour - Te Whanganui-a-Tara (The Great Harbour of Tara).

At the top station is the award winning Cable Car museum situated in the old cable car winding room and the newly opened Carter Observatory.

The Museum brings to life the story of all Wellington's iconic cable cars. It is situated within the original Winding House. It is also home to two of the original grip cars and the historic winding machinery once used to haul the cars through a series of tunnels up the steep incline. Not really my cup of tea – but interesting.

The newly refurbished Carter Observatory at the top of the hill includes a multimedia exhibition all about the Southern Skies, a planetarium, heritage telescopes and a space-themed gift shop. The Pelorus Trust Planetarium is a state of the art, digital experience that takes you on a virtual space journey, from Wellington to some of the outer regions of the Solar System. The domed theatre, has reclined seats allowing you to relax, lean back and take in the view of the sky above you, day or night.

After getting lots of photographs of Wellington from up here and visiting the museum we went for the easy downhill walk through the Botanic Gardens to Lambton Quay via the historic Bolton Street Cemetery and the Beehive. We thought this would be an enjoyable walk but we didn't realise there would be so much history to glean from it. The cemetery is a really peaceful and nostalgic place to look round and has lots of information plaques along the way.

It commemorates many early pioneers and important historical figures from the 19th Century. The Friends of Bolton Street Memorial Park (as the cemetery is now named) is a voluntary society which works closely with the Wellington City Council to preserve, protect and develop the heritage aspects of this cemetery park. It is a really interesting example of a colonial cemetery, using imported and local stone, iron and wood. Its iron memorials, wooden tablets, picket fences and wrought iron surrounds are particularly significant and comparatively rare in New Zealand.

The Chapel information centre on Bolton Street has a full burial list of the 8,679 people interred in the cemetery. This is situated alongside the Sexton's Cottage which is not open to the public but is one of the oldest surviving buildings in Wellington.

The Park itself straddles the motorway and walkways offer a unique stroll between the formal Rose Garden of the Botanic Gardens and the city centre . Memorial Trail pamphlets at each entrance enable visitors to learn of the notable people who are remembered within the Park.

Burials began formally here after 1841 when it was approved as a non-sectarian burial reserve. Deaths recorded in those early days were often a reflection of the difficulties of life for the new settlers in New Zealand. Drowning, consumption and childbirth were commonly given as causes of death. Soldiers, settlers, sailors, and especially children predominated, to be joined later by politicians and Maori and Pakeha community leaders.

In 1851 following some controversy, the 'town cemetery' was split into three sectarian areas known as Bolton Street Cemetery (for Church of England burials), Sydney Street Cemetery (the public one for "nonconformists") and the Jewish Cemetery. If you were Roman Catholic then their burials took place in the Mount Street Cemetery located adjacent to the University. You can still see these three distinct areas

There was further controversy in the 1960s over the proposed selection of the cemeteries area for the route of Wellington's motorway. A modest footbridge over the motorway was constructed and it is over this our route took us from the cemetery to the parliament buildings including the famous Beehive. It is impressive to look at but not a lot happening from the outside.

We then found ourselves on the waterfront which we followed to the Civic Square. This area was very modern and clean, and had been renovated fairly recently. The square is paved with yellow terracotta bricks and has an iconic Neil Dawson sculpture, a 3.4 metre diameter sphere using sculpted leaves of several ferns endemic to New Zealand. It is suspended 14 metres over the centre. The wide City-to-Sea pedestrian bridge is also a piece of art. It opened in 1994 and acts as a gateway from Civic Square to Wellington's waterfront at the Lagoon. The bridge is adorned with non-traditional wooden sculptures carved by prominent Māori artist Paratene Matchitt and has itself has become a tourist attraction. It was Para Matchitt's work I had admired in the Auckland Art gallery. Around the square are the Michael Fowler Centre, Wellington Town Hall, Wellington City Art Gallery and Wellington City Library.

We did pop inside the City Gallery, but not for long! We both found it hard to appreciate the art in a bookcase standing with a couple of books in, we see plenty of those at home, and the picture of a face with an old plastic bag coming out of the mouth did nothing for me. I know some people find this really interesting and meaningful but it really isn't my sort of art.

What we did enjoy though, even as much as Te Papa was the City and Sea museum.

This museum celebrates Wellington's social, cultural and maritime history. It is housed in the historic Bond Store where the original architecture complements the exhibitions. There were two particular highlights, one the Maori myths and legends show which is a dramatic 12-

minute show with special effects. We learnt about the Taniwha that created Wellington's harbour and heard how Māui tricked his grandmother into giving him fire. It was a shadow puppet show but the effects were brilliant.

The other was the story of the 1968 Wahine ferry disaster.  On 10 April 1968, the inter-island ferry, the Wahine, sailed into a savage storm and sank at the entrance to Wellington harbour. Fifty-one people died on the day and a further two people died from injuries sustained during the sinking. This dramatic documentary details the tragic event.

This museum for me was a definite must see and if I could only choose one museum to go to in Wellington I think it would be this one –it was excellent.

We wound our way back to the hotel for dinner and to pack for the following day. There were other things that we would have liked to do in Wellington such as go to Mount Victoria  a high lookout point along Wellington's Southern Walkway which gives visitors a spectacular view of the city and its surroundings or to walk along to Oriental bay and the beach. Another would be to visit the Weta Workshops which we thought about doing as we left the city, but it was in the opposite direction to Peter's so we left it. The Weta Cave is in Miramar, and it screens a behind-the-scenes look at Weta and interviews with its founders Peter Jackson, Richard Taylor, Tania Rodger and Jamie Selkirk.  In the museum, you come face to face with some of the characters, props and displays from famous movies. It is apparently a must for Lord of the Rings fans.

# *Family 2*

Saturday morning and our last week looms, don't know where the time has gone although some of those things we did in the first week or so seem a long time away now. I think we were getting a bit tired ourselves now as well. Anyway, pick up the third car from the Avis depot just down the road, we have had exactly the same car each time, a Toyota Corolla, they were very economical though. Petrol was cheaper than at home (isn't it always), but not cheap. We were paying about two dollars twenty a litre.

We set off back to Peter and Trish's. We had three nights with them and then three nights left which we had left free to decide our destination depending on what areas we felt we had not seen. The two we were thinking of were Napier and the East coast or the Coromandel peninsula. We didn't yet know of course what Peter had in store for us!!

Driving through the countryside I suddenly realised what had been missing. I hadn't seen many sheep! Remembering my geography lessons from way back I associated New Zealand with sheep farming in a big way, yet while here we had seen a lot of dairy cows but very few sheep in the fields. They also farmed much more intensely here than back home. We passed small fields absolutely crammed full of cows grazing. Dairy farming has spread rapidly, particularly in the North Island. The loss of the UK markets when Britain joined the EC was one reason but also farm subsidies began to be reduced. New Zealand's rural industries are now among the least subsidised in the world.

Other changes have also occurred, there is a lot more fruit grown now but also olives and lavender. In terms of animals deer, ostriches, emus, alpacas and goats are all now commercially produced. We saw lots of deer farms in the Fiordland area in particular.

New Zealand farmers have also responded to World concern about chemicals and food safety. Their exports of organic products have increased enormously. Farms tend to be bigger now and there are some "mega farms" owned by large companies. While we were there (January 2012) there was a lot of controversy about the selling off of many large dairy farms to the Chinese. The New Zealand government has just been ordered to review a decision allowing a Chinese company to buy 16 dairy farms on the North Island. The government had approved the sale of the 16 farms to Shanghai Pengxin saying it would help to further economic and export opportunities with China.

There were a lot of objections to this both in the papers, radio and on television. In February a New Zealand business and farming consortium which had also bid for the farms went to the High Court seeking a judicial review. It argued that the Chinese company did not offer any particular economic benefit to New Zealand and did not have the relevant experience in the dairy industry. The court appears to agree and the New Zealand government has been ordered to review the decision. I am not sure what the outcome has been but it certainly raised some issues and bad feeling at the time.

We continued to saunter up the west coast, recognising places we had previously visited such as Kapiti Island and the towns along Highway 1, places like Levin and Foxton. We were smugly beginning to feel more like locals than tourists. We arrived at Peter and Trish's for lunch and a discussion on the next few days activities.

Later that day we drove into Palmerston North and a walk in the Botanical Gardens there. Again it was very quiet although a weekend. Apart from a few joggers near the river we saw few people. The next day was going to be another long one. We decided to go over to Napier for the day. We had wanted to visit the east coast and Hawkes Bay so this was a great idea for us.

We set off early next morning through Palmerston North and over to Woodville and Dannevirke again having to detour because of the Manawhatu Gorge slip. The foothills of the Ruahine and Tararua mountain ranges to the west of Woodville host New Zealand's largest wind farm, which was established in the early 1990s and is still expanding. The prevailing westerly winds in the Manawatu-Southern Hawkes Bay region provide a consistent Median Wind Velocity which is the key relevant measure for wind generation as a renewable energy source. The Manawatu's flat pastoral lands and in particular the funnel effect created by the Manawatu Gorge in the area near Woodville are well known for being subject to high winds regularly. In the early 1990s, the newly-privatised electricity generation companies decided to site two large farms on the ridge-lines. By early 2010, as many 50 wind turbines, over 40 m in height, dotted the Tararua and Ruahine mountain ranges. Woodville now uses this fact as part of it promotion.

We stopped at the visitor centre for a huge wind farm on the way. Many people consider the wind turbines to be an eyesore and believe they are detrimental to the environmental landscape as they can be seen as far away as Palmerston North. Each to his own but they do seem quite majestic winding away on the hillside and it was certainly windy out there.

As we travelled along Highway 2 we became aware of the Scandinavian influence. The town of Dannevirke was founded on 15 October 1872 by Danish, Norwegian and Swedish settlers, who arrived at the port of Napier and moved inland. The settlers, who arrived under the Public Works Act, built their initial settlement in a clearing of the Seventy Mile Bush.

The Dannevirke after which the town was named is an extensive Viking-age fortification line. The settlement quickly earned the nickname of "sleeper town", as the town's purpose was to provide sleepers for the Napier - Wellington railway line.

Norsewood is another settlement and popular stopping place for tourists and motorists on State Highway 2. Settled in the 1870's by Scandinavian migrants Norsewood retains a unique character; children learn Scandinavian dance at school, Norway's Constitution Day is celebrated by the locals and many of the local attractions give insight into their past. There was a horse drawn cart in the street and a single petrol pump at the petrol station. It reminded me very much of Quaker settlements I had seen in America.

We arrived in Napier on a very hot Sunday. The buildings were all that we expected, fine art deco buildings that replaced those lost in the earthquake of 1931 which reached 7.8 on the Richter Scale.

Enhanced by palms and the angular Norfolk Island pines which are its trademark it is surrounded by fertile fruit and grape growing plains, dramatic hills and the shores of the South Pacific. It is the centre of the Hawke's Bay region.

Palm trees line the streets and the wonderful Marine Parade runs along the shore of the city. Along here are various parks, gardens and memorials. Known as the Art Deco City, Napier has a wonderful collection of inner-city art deco buildings. Every February, thousands of people come here to celebrate the Art Deco Weekend Summer Festival. The Festival celebrates the reconstruction of the city after the devastating earthquake. Music, performers, dancing in the street, picnics, galas and frivolity bring the 1930s back to life.

Napier is also the home of New Zealand wine, with some of the oldest wineries and wine-making establishments in the country. Some have been producing wine for over 140 years. It has some of the longest sunshine hours in New Zealand, making it a great climate for visiting, but also ideal for grape growing. Hawkes Bay generally has long hot summers as well as clear blue skies in the middle of winter. Sheltered by ranges to the west the area around Hawkes Bay is dominated by rolling hills and fertile plains. This is the perfect environment for orchards and the internationally acclaimed wineries of this area. Whatever time of the year you visit, you're pretty much guaranteed to have dry sunny weather.

It was certainly a baking hot day when we visited. It is New Zealand's second-largest wine region, leading the country with 70% of Cabernet Sauvignon and 30% of Chardonnay production. There are lots of different wine tours to choose, from boutique wineries to major operations.

We found a lovely street cafe for lunch and followed this with a walk along the beach. The weather was clear and you could see the whole spread of this enormous bay. Being a weekend there were lots of people on the beach busy with activities of one type or another. Many were walking, biking, riding, playing games – very few were actually just sitting. This seemed to be typical of many of the coastal areas we had visited. New Zealanders are very into outdoor activities which are well catered for with lots of skate board parks and facilities for outdoorsy types of sports

We then drove out to Cape Kidnappers. This is a headland marking the south-eastern extremity of Hawkes Bay where 100m tall jagged rock formations protrude from the ocean at the end of the 8km peninsula. It is south-east of Napier. The cape is a short drive of about twenty Kilometres. The Cape Kidnappers Golf Course, one of over 20 in the region, is rated in the top 50 golf courses in the world. The course is located on the Cape's northern cliff-edge, and looks out across the whole of Hawkes Bay, with stunning views over Napier to the mountain ranges beyond and across 80km of the Pacific Ocean towards the Mahia Peninsula.

The headland was named after an attempt by local Māori to abduct the servant of a member of Captain Cook's crew aboard HMS Endeavour in 1769. The crew member was Tiata, a Tahitian accompanying Cook's interpreter Tupaia. Cook's journal states that Tiata was in the water near Endeavour when a Māori fishing boat pulled alongside and dragged him aboard. Sailors from Endeavour's deck immediately opened fire on the fishing boat, killing two Māori and wounding a third. Tiata promptly jumped overboard and swam back to Endeavour, while the remaining Māori paddled their craft back to shore. A 4-pounder cannon was fired after them from Endeavour's quarterdeck, but the Māori boat was soon out of range.

Cook described the cape as having steep white cliffs on either side, with two large rocks resembling hay stacks near the headland. Certainly looking towards Cape Kidnappers from Napier it looks very much like the white cliffs of Dover. It is also home to over 3000 pairs of gannets. When you visit you can get within a few feet of the world's largest, most accessible mainland gannet colony which is at the top of the Cape's sheer and barren cliffs.

After this we had a visit to Hastings to pick up some new family members. Trish had bought some baby rabbits and we were to pick them up from here before returning home. We spent a fair bit of the journey thinking up silly names for them!

It seemed a long journey back and was indeed quite late when we got in and we were all tired after dinner. The following day the plan was to go to further up the west coast to New Plymouth.

Got up to make a cup of tea next morning feeling absolutely shattered. Being so busy all the time was beginning to catch up with us. We weren't sure if we were up to another full day with lots of driving. Met Peter in the kitchen making tea and fortunately he said they were both tired from all the driving the day before. So we decided to have a leisurely breakfast, Jeff and I would look round Bulls and then we would go for a walk nearby later in the day. This seemed to suit us all fine. So we went back to bed with our tea and caught up with our e-mails, postcards etc. We sent lots of postcards and I have to admit that Jeff wrote most of them. We also looked on the Internet for places to stay for the next few days. As we had been to Napier we decided we would make our way north on the west side of north island which we had not seen and then have our final couple of nights in the Coromandel. We are eBay users at home and we spent some time having a look at their equivalent which is Trade Me - it works in exactly the same way.

We sauntered into Bulls and got provisions for the evening. There is a very nice bookshop in Bulls that had a lot of old books about New Zealand. One thing we noticed all over New Zealand was that books, whether new or old were very expensive over there. They were at least double the price they are here, mainly because they all have to be imported.

Bulls is actually named after James Bull, a carpenter from Chelsea in London who was only 26 when he came to New Zealand. He travelled on the Indian Queen in 1857. In 1858 he went off with a long time friend of his Dick Howard who was going to build a new ferry house and hotel for Thomas Scott at the mouth of the Rangitikei River. While there he met Christina, one of Thomas Scott's four daughters and they were married in 1859.

He operated all sorts of businesses in the area over time and was a great citizen of the growing township, so it was inevitable that it became known as going to Bull's. It was in 1872 that the name of Bulls was officially accepted by the Post Office. Until then it had various names, Daniells Bush, Middle Rangitikei, Clifton, Taumaihi and Bulltown. He retired from all his enterprises in 1900 and returned to his home town of Chelsea in England where he died in 1920 aged 89.

At least Bulls was an easy name to remember, write and say unlike some of the names we encountered. The previous day in southern Hawkes Bay we had been near the town with longest place name in any English speaking country — Taumatawhakatangihangakoauauotamateaturipukakapiki maungahoronukupokaiwhenuakitanatahu. It is listed in the Guiness book of records and the sign itself is ten metres long. Translated it means " the brow of the hill on which Tamatea, who sailed the whole country, played the nose flute for his beloved".

The next day we were leaving Bulls and having to say goodbye to family which was rather sad as we don't know when we will see them again and they had arranged so much for us during our visit. We had decided to travel as far as Whatawhata (as we had found what looked like an interesting bed and breakfast place here), and then we were going up to the Coromandel the following day. It was still going to be a drive of just over four hundred kilometres but through areas we had not yet travelled.

# *North to Coromandel*

We took Highway 3 to Wanganui and then Highway 4 north. The drive began through farmland and river scenery, then from Wanganui it wandered through a world of rivers and gentle but densely covered hill country. On Highway 4, thirty kilometres south of Raetihi are the Rauwaka Falls. This is an attractively wide waterfall that's approximately 15m tall and 50m wide. It's easily found as there is a signed pull in along the main highway. From here you go to a viewing platform that allows you to look below at the impressive waterfall in the distance. It is worth checking out if you're in the area.

The landscape then became more volcanic as we neared the National Park Village. This is a small settlement well positioned for exploring the Tongariro National Park. Apparently all three volcanic peaks can be seen from here but once again we had low cloud and didn't manage to see them!! It would seem you need to be prepared for extreme weather changes in this national park as it can transition from fine and warm to windy, wet and cold quite suddenly.

Travelling north towards the rural town of Te Kuiti, which hosts NZ sheep shearing championships each year, we drove through an area of farmland known as the 'King Country'.

The name King Country comes from the Māori King Movement that began in 1850 as a response to the arrival of large numbers of British settlers seeking land and the purchase of land by the Colonial government from various Maori Tribes. It is named after the Maori warrior Chief "King Tawhiao", who with his determined followers led a resistance to the Europeans. The King country is a huge area - the size of Belgium, and was a no go area for Europeans for approximately 20 years. The area today is still largely covered in heavy bush. Ventures by farmers to farm the area in the 1920s were abandoned along with the famous "Bridge to Nowhere" that can only be reached by tramping for several hours. The official residence of the Kings and Queens is the Maori National Assembly House near Hamilton towards which we were driving.

The fairly recent death of the Maori Queen Dame Te Atairangikaahu in May 2006 will long be remembered as a momentous occasion in the history of New Zealand. It is estimated 100,000 mourners travelled to Ngaruawhaia to pay their respects to Dame Te Ata in the biggest funeral this generation of New Zealanders is likely to see. Although the new monarch did not necessarily have to be a member of the Tainui tribe as were the previous six, the council of chiefs named Dame Te Ata's eldest son, Tuheiti Paki as seventh leader of the Kingitanga movement. In keeping with tradition their decision was announced on the day of internment to ensure the spirit of the tribe is not broken. The new king was welcomed onto the marae by a paramount chief and the crowd asked if they accepted him to be king. "Ae" they replied. Mr Paki then sat on the elaborately carved throne where after being tapped on the head with a bible he was proclaimed King.

Travel Tip: Find out about the current Maori King Tuheiti Paki.

Continuing north towards the Waitomo Caves we came to the river town of Taumaranui, from where you can start lots of Whanganui River activities.

The area known as Waitomo Caves is then only a short drive from Te Kuiti. Beneath the surface of this ancient limestone landscape is a series of vast cave systems that are well known for their stalactites, stalagmites and glow-worms. Wai means water, tomo means hole. When put together you have the perfect name for a region that's full of limestone caves.

The trip onward to Hamilton took us through prime Waikato farmland. There is a kiwi house in Otorohanga where there is a chance to meet New Zealand's national symbols or you can detour towards the west coast to Kawhia, where hot water bubbles up through the sand and you can dig a pool between low and mid tide. We never did see a Kiwi. Kiwi has three meanings in New Zealand, the flightless bird, the little green fruit and anyone with a New Zealand passport. There is no disrespect in this term and they are proud of the name.

We were on the look out though for our guest house as we only had a rough idea where it was. We knew it was on the edge of Whatawhata, but we seemed to be on a new estate with huge, beautiful, individually built houses with lots of land. It didn't exactly look like a bed and breakfast area! We had seen a picture of the house on the website and it was quite distinctive so we knew what we were looking for. Then suddenly I saw the Italianate arches across the countryside so we made our way across to it. We were soon there and being welcomed into the most beautiful house. Beaumere is in a wonderful country setting with magic views and sunsets over the Hakaramata Ranges, a perfect place to relax.

It was a fabulous house, we were in our own wing with our own garden area, patio table and chairs and best of all a hot tub in the garden which we were invited to use - and we did. We settled in and then went for a little walk around the area and then Peter, (one of the owners) asked if we would like a drink, so we joined him for wine and snacks in their lounge. It was interesting listening to his account of his fairly recent visit to England. His wife's family were substantial landowners in England in the past and they were looking up old haunts. He was disappointed Jeff didn't play golf as he wanted to whisk him off to the golf course. The following morning Isobel cooked us a very tasty hot breakfast before going off to golf. Everything was fresh and cooked to order, the preserves homemade and really delicious. It was certainly a great find.

We only had a short drive that day to Thames so we decided on the advice of our hosts to drive out west to Raglan first.

Raglan is the perfect escape from the hustle and bustle of everyday life, whether you're looking for world-class surf, stunning scenery, beautiful beaches, inspiring arts or simply a good old cup of coffee. Situated on the coast it is fast becoming a busy holiday destination both for New Zealanders and international visitors. It is surrounded by water and bush and overlooked by the majestic Mount Karioi. There are said to be breathtaking views from every corner (but it was raining when we arrived). The town was judged to be "New Zealand's "Best Looking Town" by Lonely Planet guidebooks. The black volcanic sands of Ngaranui beach, just a few kilometres from the town are popular for surfing, bodyboarding, swimming and walking. In surfing terms it apparently has three world-class Point Breaks! There are also spectacular views from the top of Mount Karioi, but it's a three hour trek to get there.

The town was the scene for a very public civil disobedience campaign in the 1970s. During World War II the New Zealand Government took local ancestral land from indigenous Māori owners to construct a military airfield. When this was no longer required for defence purposes, part of the land was not returned to the owners but became the public Raglan golf course.

There was widespread protest and attempts to reoccupy the land, and in 1978 twenty Māori protesters were arrested on the ninth hole of the golf course. The land was eventually returned to the owners.

We had a look around the town and went to the newly re-opened museum. The building it is now in was only completed in August 2011. It had a lot of information on local history for the Raglan area and adjacent districts. Many of the artefacts illustrate domestic, rural and town life in Raglan, mainly during the early twentieth century. There are lots of old photographs and many early copies of the town's newspaper, The Raglan County Chronicle.

The elegant, historic, colonial Harbour View Hotel was a good place for coffee before we set off for Thames at the base of the Coromandel Peninsula.

We returned to Hamilton and across to Morrinsville and Te Aroha before arriving in Thames and finding our accommodation. We had a choice of chalets which was nice. They were spacious, with quite a large kitchen area and views out to the sea on the Firth of Thames. We were very pleasantly surprised as it had looked quite ordinary on the website. After unpacking we went for a walk along the beach. There were lots of sea birds in flocks and interesting tide lines to explore.

Thames is a great base for visiting the Coromandel Peninsula. Most places on the Coromandel are within 1 to 1.5 hours drive from here and there's lots to keep you busy.

It is known as the "Gateway to the Coromandel Peninsula" and it was certainly that for us. It is the main shopping centre for the area and as well as the numerous varied speciality shops it has an historic main street and the modern Goldfields Shopping Mall. Thames in the late 19th century was one of New Zealand's largest towns, and in fact was even considered as a site for the capital, built on the pioneering industries of gold and Kauri logging. Its colourful history is still alive in the pubs, buildings and museums of the area and it has absolutely fantastic forests and coastlines.

We had one full day so we planned to go up the west coast to Coromandel Town. We ended up touring the whole of the peninsula as it made sense having already driven north. The road was narrow and ran very close to the edge of the sea which was fine apart from the numerous tight bends and the logging trucks! The two just don't go together.

We stopped at the Mussel Kitchen for a coffee. The Kitchen is unique in that they collect, cultivate, harvest, cook and serve their own green lipped mussels thus controlling freshness, flavour and quality. You can enjoy Coromandel's fresh mussels, watch some hand- made culinary products being prepared and buy some to take away.

Young mussels, known as 'Spat', bind onto seaweed off the West Coast of Northland. During storms or when the sea is rough the seaweed breaks off the seabed and washes up naturally onto 90 mile beach. The seaweed is then collected and transported to the Coromandel. After being cultivated they are harvested 3-5 times per week to ensure maximum freshness and flavour.

Sadly we only had coffee as it was mid morning. They have events there too and later that day there was a jazz evening with food which sounded brilliant.

It was only another five minute drive to Coromandel Town. Coromandel is the name of the town and harbour. The town was named after the peninsula, which was named after HMS Coromandel, which sailed into the harbour in 1820.

The discovery of gold at Driving Creek in 1852 brought a boom to Coromandel Town, and the area has continued to flourish while retaining much of its history from those times. It became a major port serving both the gold mining and kauri industries.

The kauri is the most famous of NZ timbers. It has the largest trunk girth of any native tree ranging from 10 - 15 feet. Dense kauri forest once covered large areas of north Auckland and the Coromandel Peninsula. Europeans exploited most of this resource by the mid 1920's. What is left is now protected. The Maori of the far north used kauri for their canoes and for carving panels for meeting houses. Europeans used kauri for almost everything from masts on sailing ships, panelling, flooring and furniture.

The Kauri tree was in demand as it has a long straight trunk which is relatively free of side branches and this made it easy to mill. The logs were flushed out of the valleys, sometimes thousands at a time. Purpose built dams were built to provide the push and by the 1870s three quarters of the kauri trees were already gone!

Today, the main industries are tourism and mussel farming.

Coromandel Harbour is a wide bay on the Hauraki Gulf. There are several islands just off the coast, the largest of which is Whanganui Island. This makes for some very photogenic viewpoints. You can't help but be moved by the beauty of the lush undergrowth, the beaches and the islands sparkling in the sun. You can see why it is a popular summer holiday destination for New Zealanders. Coromandel is noted for its artists, crafts, alternative lifestylers, mussel farming, and fishing. Many talented artists and craftspeople from around the country are inspired not only by the tranquil atmosphere, but also by the spectacular natural surroundings.

It was an interesting town to look round. Some of the craft shops have some really unusual and eye catching items. Jeff bought me a bangle in one of them. We saw a lovely painting that we were tempted by but would have needed to have it shipped home and decided against it in the end. There are lots of interesting buildings as you walk around and there are both heritage and craft trail booklets containing further information. The I-site has a particular wealth of information and many booklets too.

We had seen signs for the Auckland ferry as we approached the town and a new ferry service is now established between Downtown Auckland and Coromandel Town. The ferry takes you through the most scenic part of the Huraki Gulf and therefore opens up the area more for visitors from overseas.

It was as we were leaving Coromandel Town that we decided we might as well drive all the way round the peninsula as there was a lot to see on the eastern side too. We set off but stopped at Kuaotunu. It is a beautiful coastal village and the beach looked inviting. The Kuaotunu bay is also a popular place for friendly dolphins who frequently stop here to play in the bay.

There was only one couple there and we had a chat. They were from Auckland and were house sitting for a friend (I could do that job)! They described lots of places we might like to stop off at as we continued our route back to Thames. The first of these was hot water beach. We continued along to Whitianga a busy town where we got sandwiches and drinks for a picnic later.

We turned off for Hot Water Beach, ignoring the signs to Cooks Beach.

When Captain Cook visited the Coromandel in 1769, he thought he had arrived in heaven and stayed quite a few days. He raised the Union Jack in NZ for the first time, probably at a site near Cook's Beach, adjacent to the entrance of the Purangi Estuary in the Stella Evered Park. The land at that time was covered in luxuriant forests thick with enormous trees and lush undergrowth right to the water's edge.

Hot Water Beach is approximately 12 kilometres south of Whitianga. It has underground hot springs which filter up through the sand between the high and low water tides. The beach is popular with locals and tourists. Within two hours either side of low tide, it is possible to dig into the sand allowing hot water to escape to the surface forming a hot water pool. The water, with a temperature as hot as 64°C, filters up from two underground fissures located close to each other. These natural springs can be found on the beach opposite the off-shore rocks. People dig large holes and relax and soak in the thermal water. You can hire spades from the nearby surf shop if you don't take one with you. Unfortunately the tide was wrong when we were there.

Hot Water Beach also has dangerous rip currents and large waves. Signs at the beach advise swimmers not to swim within 50m either side of the off-shore rocks. Hot Water Beach's rip currents have claimed the lives of several unfortunate visitors and only strong and experienced swimmers are advised to enter the water. It was an interesting place with information boards explaining the phenomena in detail.

We then continued to nearby Cathedral Cove. We parked at the local authority car park at the top of the headland between Hahei and Gemstone Bay. The area is very popular with tourists, and receives around 150,000 visitors a year. There was also a great craft co-operative there to look round.

Te Whanganui-A-Hei (Cathedral Cove) is a marine reserve. It is named after the cave located there linking Mare's Leg Cove to Cathedral Cove. Gemstone Bay and Stingray Bay are also accessible from here. A walking track exists from the local authority car park at the top of the headland to Cathedral Cove. We found the car park really busy and had to drive around a while before we got a parking space. It was a marvellous day and the views from the hilltop were incredible.

We set off along the track  detouring  to Gemstone bay which was interesting . It is a rocky and popular snorkelling bay with boards giving information about what you might see in the water. We then returned to the one hour walking track leading to the stunningly beautiful Cathedral Cove. Here a gigantic arched cavern passes through a white rock headland joining two secluded coves. It is a place with an air of grandeur. The beach is beautifully sandy with pohutukawa trees near the shore. A perfect place except for all the tourists! It's  Māori name is Te Whanganui-A-Hei (the Great Bay of Hei). The cave and beach was also used as the tunnel through which the Pevensie children first re-enter Narnia in the movie version of The Chronicles of Narnia. Yes it is spectacular but I preferred those solitary beaches back in the Abel Tasman National Park.

The drive back to Thames wound through the forests and hills of the Coromandel Forest to the Kaueranga Valley. The Kauaeranga River was once named

Waiwhakauaeranga, which means "waters of the stacked-up jaw bones". It is claimed the name originated from a famous battle when members of Ngati Maru stacked up the jaw bones of their defeated enemies in rows on the banks of the river.

This beautiful area includes 21 walking tracks ranging from 20 minute strolls to rewarding overnight trails. It is an ideal area for hikers, mountain bikers and nature lovers. The rugged hills, which include Table Mountain (846 metres) and the Pinnacles (759 metres), provide spectacular views.

Since the early logging in the 1900's the forest has been regenerating for the last eighty years and there are now kauri, rimu, totara, kahikatea and kowhai trees, as well as a wide range of ferns. Needless to say there are lots of native bird species seen and heard throughout the area.

We called in at a restaurant in Thames to book a table as this was our last night out in New Zealand as we would be in the airport hotel the following night.

It was rather sad coming to the last day of our holiday in New Zealand. We took the coast road to Auckland rather than the main road. This was nearly a mistake, we encountered a lot of traffic coming in the opposite direction as there was a pop festival being held there that weekend and had it been later in the day it looked as though we may have got caught in heavy traffic.

The coast road takes you through an area renowned for its bird life. We passed the Miranda hot springs and the Shorebird Centre but stopped at a couple of quiet beaches along the way.

As we got nearer to Auckland we were obviously in riding territory passing lots of stud farms and polo clubs. We arrived at the Novotel airport hotel in the early afternoon. It seemed very ordinary after the lovely places we had stayed in over the past month. We had some serious sorting to do. We needed to offload what we no longer needed but also had to sort what we wanted for our overnight stay in South Korea as our bags were going straight through to London. As if the weather realised we were at the end of the holiday it started to rain and then turned into a full blown thunder storm. Unfortunately it flooded the pool area where I had hoped to go and read a book later in the sun. It reappeared as a beautiful red sunset later that evening.

Packed, showered, fed and reminiscing about what a fabulous time we had experienced we had an early night as we had to be at the airport at 6am having dropped off the car. While in New Zealand we had driven over three thousand miles!

Travel Tip: When hiring a car make sure you get unlimited mileage.

*Lesley Gould*

# South Korea and Home

Check in was quick and uneventful except as always Jeff had to be searched as his hip replacement always starts the scanner off. I get used to waiting for him in airports.

The plane was on time and again we could not fault Korean Air. The service was excellent and I have never been on a flight where the toilets are cleaned so often! So we were heading for our overnight stay in South Korea.

In Korean mythology there is a story about how the Korean nation was born. The story is that a god named Hwanung came from heaven and transformed a bear into a woman. He married her and she gave birth to a son, Tangun, the founder of Korea. Tangun created the first capital of the Korean nation in 2333 B.C and called it Joseon - 'Land of the Morning Calm'. I love these names and it felt right to be travelling from the Land of the Long White Cloud to the Land of the Morning Calm.

South Korea is noted for its population density, which is 487 per square kilometre, more than 10 times the global average. The population has also been shaped by international migration. After World War II and the division of the Korean Peninsula, about four million people from North Korea crossed the border to South Korea. This trend of net entry reversed over the next 40 years due to emigration, especially to the United States and Canada.

The airport is actually at Incheon, west of Seoul. Incheon International Airport was opened in 2001 due to the demand for light transportation services and is now a hub airport for Northeast Asia and its airport is world renowned. It was built on reclaimed land between Yeongjongdo Island and Yongudo Island. It accommodates supersonic speed and super-large aircraft. It has an annual turnover of twenty eight million passengers and twenty three million tons of freight. It is very proud to be ranked as "World No. 1 for airport services" and "No 2 for International freight services". It was a fantastic airport with a huge shopping Mall inside. It has overnight accommodation, restaurants, a Traditional Culture Experience for passengers to try out different crafts among its many facilities. It has 132 different gates to fly out from, we had walked for ages to walk to the one we needed on the way out.

At the airport after going through immigration we had to meet at the Korean Air desk where we were assigned hotels for the night. We were also given dinner and breakfast vouchers and one for lunch at the airport the following day as the flight was not until early afternoon.

We assembled with about ten others and were taken by coach to the Harbour Park Hotel a downtown hotel that gives a panoramic view of the ocean to the west and Chinatown to the east. We crossed over to it on the incredible Incheon Bridge which looked spectacular lit up at night.

The Incheon Metropolitan City is located in the northwest of South Korea. Today 2.76 million people live in the city, making it Korea's third most populous city after Seoul and Busan Metropolitan City.

In 2003, the city was designated as Korea's first free economic zone. Since then, large local companies and global enterprises have increasingly invested in Incheon including Samsung.

South Korea's education system is technologically advanced and it is the world's first country to bring high-speed fibre-optic broadband internet access to every primary and secondary school nation-wide. Using this infrastructure, the country has developed the first Digital Textbooks in the world, which will be distributed for free to every primary and secondary school nation-wide by 2013. Plans of creating English-teaching robot assistants to compensate for the shortage of teachers were announced in February 2010, with the robots being deployed to most preschools and kindergartens by 2013. Robotics are also incorporated in the entertainment sector as well; the Korean Robot Game Festival has been held every year since 2004 to promote science and robot technology.

It has led the economic development of Korea since opening its port to the outside world. As an international city, Incheon has held numerous large scale international conferences. The 17th Asian Games " Incheon 2014" will also be held here from September 19, that year.

Our hotel overlooked the port area. It has the largest Floodgate in Asia and facilities that can dock up to seventy vessels. The International Passenger Terminal is often swarming with passengers travelling between China and Incheon. The international car ferries connect seven major cities in China.

We had a lovely hot and cold buffet meal at the hotel along with many other travellers who were also in transit and who were flying off to different destinations the next day. The bedroom, as you would expect in Korea was very high tech. The lighting came on and off by movement and the toilet/bidet needed a manual! The seat was heated (three different levels), and you could have roving jets, still ones, blow dry, soft jets, medium or fast jets!!!! At least the instructions were in Korean and English and I did try it out!

The following morning we had a superb breakfast with all imaginable hot and cold foods. I tried out some ramboutan for the first time ever. Rambutan is a tropical fruit from Asia and belongs to the same family as the lychee. They contain many nutrients including vitamin C and glucose. Although ugly looking little fruits they were actually very soft and sweet inside. The dining room was at the top of the hotel and had huge picture windows so you admire the view.

Our flight was not until early afternoon so we had a free morning. As we were not being collected until lunch time we went for a walk around the area near the hotel. It was still very cold and there was snow around in piles where it had been cleared. The temperature had been minus seven degrees when we arrived the night before. Immediately behind the hotel was the Korean Chinese Cultural Centre, a very decorative building. It acts as a mediator of exchange between Korea and China to help the understanding of the different cultures of both countries.

We also passed the Boundary Stairs between the Qing and Japanese Settlements. These were stone stairs leading up the hill between the two settlements to a pagoda type building at the top. Each side of the steps is

landscaped and is designed so that the steep stairs can be used to enjoy the surrounding scenery. At the upper part of the stairs is a statue of Confucius. As we were near Chinatown we saw the Paeru, the traditional Chinese Gate across the entrance of the main street. Another of these

was opposite the hotel. The architecture is both elaborate and beautiful. We passed the Euiseon-dang, a temple intended for the edification of Chinese and the Hanjungwon, an outdoor cultural space.

As we returned to the hotel towards the port we saw a huge monument which had been built in 1986 to commemorate the 100th anniversary of Christianity in Korea. If staying longer there are many cultural tours you can do in Incheon with historic themed tours based on China, Japan and Korea as well as other countries too.

We travelled back to the airport with great views of the bridge and back to the port area. As we had only hand luggage we were quick to get through security and had been given our boarding passes the day before. We found the Korean Cultural Experience Centre at the airport where you can make traditional arts and crafts, explore Korean music and costume and a lovely gift shop. We had to go and find out the exchange rate to work out approximately how much the items cost. They were inexpensive and we could use our credit card so bought a few lovely items. One pound sterling is equivalent to 1800 South Korean Won!

So the holiday is virtually over. The plane almost left on time, we were all aboard but had to wait for flight time to be available over China.

One of the meals we did try during the flight was the Bibimbap. This is a signature Korean dish. The word literally means "mixed meal" or "mixed rice". It is served as a bowl of warm white rice topped with sautéed and seasoned vegetables and a chilli  pepper paste. The ingredients all came in little pots and these are stirred together thoroughly just before eating. You were given an A4 sheet of instructions on how to prepare it (as you had to do this yourself), and it can be served either cold or hot.

Despite our slightly late departure, we still arrived at Heathrow on time and our son Andy and girlfriend Mel were there to meet us. Back up the motorway to Derby and that was it. I never like going home at the end of a holiday and this was no exception. It had been an experience to remember though. There were so many highlights and so much more I wanted to find out about which takes us back to the start and  how this book started, and once started I couldn't stop.

I find the end of holidays very difficult. Although I love family and home I rarely want a holiday to end and am in my element planning the next trip. I did have an added incentive this time though of looking forward to seeing our granddaughter again and seeing how she had changed.

There aren't many countries that I would want to live in but I think New Zealand might be one of them. In general spring comes earlier to New Zealand, summer lasts longer and autumn comes later, therefore the winters are shorter, warmer and sunnier than the UK unless you live in the mountains.

As we both love the countryside and walking we enjoyed the stunning and varied scenery. It's wildness and majesty are such that you just look in awe. The deserted beaches and thick native forests are just fabulous. Here we found solitude and a real sense of wilderness.

If I manage to return one day I would like to see more of the eastern side of both islands. The East Cape is said to be very wild and unspoilt though less dramatic than some of the sights we had seen. I'd like to explore the Raukamara Mountains and stand in the first place in the world to see the sun rise on a new day. To visit the Urewara National Park which has the largest tract of untouched native forest in North Island would be on my wish list. I would like to spend time in the Blenheim area and see the yellow eyed penguins in the Otago Peninsula. The more I find out the more I want to see.

I have enjoyed writing about my travels in New Zealand and reliving my experiences and I hope you enjoy reading it either for pleasure or as part of planning your own trip. If you do go you can't fail to be impressed.

Sadly I now need to go and do some housework (secret code for planning the next trip)!

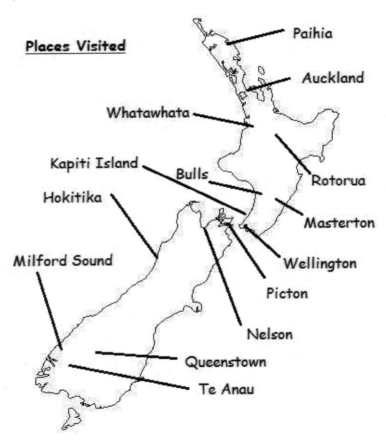

**Places Visited**

Paihia
Auckland
Whatawhata
Kapiti Island
Bulls
Rotorua
Hokitika
Masterton
Milford Sound
Wellington
Picton
Nelson
Queenstown
Te Anau

# *List of Illustrations*

Chapter 6 - Fiordland

Garston Hotel, en route to Te Anau

Trips and Tramps minibus

Sign on the road to Milford Sound

Homer Tunnel

Milford Sound

Key Summit


Chapter 7 – The West Coast

Arrowtown, Chinese Settlement

Cardrona Hotel, Cardrona

Wooden Building, Cardrona

Thunder Creek Falls

Hokitika Beach

Seats, Hokitika

One way bridge


Chapter 8 - Abel Tasman Coast

Water Taxi Stands, Kaiteriteri

Split Apple Rock

Beach, Abel Tasman coast track

The Mussel Pot, Havelock

100<sup>th</sup> Anniversary of Christianity in Korea

Incheon Airport


Map of places visited

Sketches produced from original photographs using InstaSketch free app.

*Lesley Gould*

# *Transport and Accomodation Details*

Flights to and from New Zealand via Seoul with Korean Air.

Internal flight from Wellington to Queenstown with Air New Zealand.

Ferry from Picton to Wellington with Interislander.

Car hire Avis New Zealand for each car.

Accommodation in order of travel :

Rendezvous Hotel, Vincent Street, Auckland

Garden Suite, Craicor, Paihia, bay of Islands.

The Herb Garden, Te Kauwhata

Victoria Lodge, Victoria Street, Rotarua.

The Village Inn, Te Anau

The Goldridge Resort, Frankton Road, Queenstown

The Garden Bed and Breakfast, Fitzherbert Street, Hokitika

The Honest Lawyer, Nelson

Glengary Bed and Breakfast, Seaview Crescent, Picton

Abel Tasman Hotel, Willis Street, Wellington.

Beaumere Lodge, Whatawhata

Coastal Motor Lodge, Thames.

Holiday Inn, Auckland Airport

Harbour View Hotel, Incheon.